Why Can't **You** Communicate Like **Me**?

How Smart Women Get Results at Work

Laura Browne

IN YOUR FACE INK, LLC

Glendale, Arizona · 2005

In Your Face Ink, LLC
www.inyourfaceink.com

In Your Face Ink, LLC
9524 W. Camelback Road
#130-182
Glendale, AZ 85305
Tel: (623) 570-1072
www.inyourfaceink.com

Printed in the United States of America
First Printing: May 2005
ISBN 0-9765659-0-0
Library of Congress Control Number on file.
Browne, Laura.
Why Can't You Communicate Like Me?
/ by Laura Browne
1. Communication. 2. Women.
3. Business   4. Career.

Front Cover:
Model: Jill L. Ferguson
Hair and Makeup: Maria Reid
Photography: James Reid
Design and Typesetting: Edward J. Kamholz

Why Can't **You** Communicate Like **Me?**

How Smart Women Get Results at Work

Acknowledgements

This book would not have been possible without the generous help from many terrific people. Special thanks to:

My husband, Duncan, & daughter, Julie, and all my family and friends for their love and support.

Howard, for helping me to get started.

My writing group: Jill, Margie, Vandy, Heather, Debbie, Linda, and Julie for their tremendous help and encouragement.

Jean Otte, Rosina Racioppi, Amy Gonzales, and the rest of the wonderful WOMEN Unlimited gang for inspiring me and so many other women to take risks and nurture the growth of others.

Contents

I
Introduction

I   Succeeding at Work

Do you want to create better relationships at work, take charge of your career, learn a systematic approach to dealing with others, have more fun and become more successful? Then you need to learn how to be a more effective communicator.

You probably get along well with some people at work. Other people are more difficult and sometimes those problem people can include your boss or major customers. In order to be successful, it's not enough to get along with the people you like; you need to be able to work well with everyone. This book shows you how to look at the way you communicate with others and how to use that information to move ahead in your career.

The key to communicating with other people is to find out how THEY like to get and give information. By being aware of their preferences, you can talk in ways that they can best understand.

This is because people communicate in different ways. Some people are surprised to hear this idea. They assume that everyone gets and gives information exactly like they do. When they have problems with someone, they think that the other person is just being stupid or rude. But when they understand the 4 B model, they realize that other people aren't being annoying on purpose, they're just doing what makes the most sense to them.

You know that some people talk more than you do and some talk less. There are people you work with who are faster paced and jump into projects and others who appear more patient or who need more time to think before acting. You know this, but underneath, you may be thinking that we're all people so we all should communicate the same way.

By understanding how other people like to relate to others, you can communicate with them more easily. Think of it as learning new languages. If you know that someone else's native language is Spanish, communication would be much easier if you could learn Spanish. It's the same with communication types. If you are communicating with someone who speaks a different language, you will get along better with her if you learn that language.

Let's look at the four main ways that women communicate at work: the 4 Bs. You can remember them by the easily recognizable terms of Bossy, Bubbly, Buddy, and Brainy. Don't get put off by the terms; we're going to use them to better understand how different women get their points across. These terms refer to methods of communication, not to personality. Even though personality influences communication, personality defines who you are on a more basic level. For this book's purpose, we're going to focus on understanding how people's communication types affect how they interact with others.

Women who are direct and clearly say what they want communicate in the Bossy type. They appear to be confident and tell others what to do. They talk quickly and get right to the point.

Women who are friendly and creative communicate in the Bubbly type. They focus on the positive aspects of situations and use words to motivate others. They may use humor and tell jokes.

Women who ask about other people's feelings communicate in the Buddy type. They are good listeners and people often confide in them. They take the time to make sure everyone's opinions are included.

Women who are quiet and methodical communicate in the Brainy style. They speak in a structured manner. They carefully consider their message before they say it.

Do you recognize the women you work with in those descriptions? Do you recognize yourself? You may see a little bit of yourself in all of the descriptions. That's to be expected since we're all complex individuals. Typically though, you'll find that you are most comfortable with one or possibly two of the descriptions. When you understand where you are most at ease, you can begin to see why you get along with some people and not with others. Usually you get along best with people who like to communicate the same way you do.

HOW DO OTHERS SEE YOU AT WORK?

If you want to move up in the organization and become more valuable, you need to get along with everyone. You can't control anyone else's perceptions of you, but you can control how you present yourself. Once you understand how people see you, you can make some small changes in the way you work so you can get better results.

You don't have to become a totally different person or do anything that you don't agree with. But you may have to learn some new ways of talking to people to make sure that they understand you.

You're going to limit your potential for success if you only communicate clearly with people who are like you. Unfortunately, you often can't choose your co-workers, boss, employees and customers. You need to be prepared to work well with everyone, whether you're comfortable or you're not.

WHAT THIS MEANS FOR YOU

As a trainer, I have shared this knowledge in different versions at workshops with hundreds of people across the country. Participants have told me that understanding this information has positively changed how they deal with others. It works. And it can work for you. To help you see how you can use it, I've included four case studies at the end of the chapters for you to follow. These examples will help you to see how to get the results you want.

HOW WE'RE GOING TO DO THIS

First you need to understand how you like to communicate. Take the following brief quiz to help you determine which type describes you most closely. This information will help you to understand why you get along with some people and not with others. It will also give you insight into actions that you'll need to take in order to work better with people whose communication skills aren't like yours.

When you calculate the scores, some of you may be surprised because you don't think of yourself in that way. You may even be offended by the label (such as Bubbly type). Don't be put off by the titles. Read the descriptions with an open mind to get the most out of this.

Some people aren't surprised at all by their scores. They think their behavior is so obvious that they can figure it out even without the quiz.

When you read through the section of the book that describes your type, ask yourself how closely it matches how you usually communicate. Of course, everyone is unique so not all of the information will be correct, but you should find the overall description accurate.

4B QUIZ

Read each comment and choose the answer that most closely describes how you act or feel at work. Please choose only one answer for each question. If more than one answer accurately describes you, go with your first instinct. Put your answers on the answer sheet at the end of the quiz.

    1. When I start something new at work, I:
        a) Make a list of all the things I need to do
        b) Ask someone else for suggestions
        c) Brainstorm some ideas of how to do it

d) Decide on the quickest way to get it done

2. When I have to tell someone bad news, I:

a) Tell them

b) Tell them to look at the bright side and I point out the positives

c) Worry how the other person will feel about the bad news so I talk it over with someone else to help me prepare

d) Carefully explain all the reasons so they can understand the logic behind the news

3. When I'm working with a group of people, I:

a) Keep things on track so there are no delays

b) Make sure that everyone gets included in the information so no one feels left out

c) Suggest ways to keep people interested and enthusiastic

d) Make sure that procedures are followed so nothing is missed

4. When I show someone else how to do a task, I:

a) Show them as quickly as possible so I can get back to my work

b) Explain the Standard Operating Procedure, and make sure they understand all the steps to do it correctly

c) I get them excited about the task so they'll want to do it

d) Chat with them so they're comfortable and then help them to learn the task at their own speed

5. On Monday morning one of the first things I do is:

a) Ask how other people spent their weekend

b) Tell people how I spent my weekend

c) Look at my to-do list and plan my day

d) Get to work

6. If I'm mad at someone at work, I:

a) Tell them

b) Try to avoid them

    c) Smooth it over—I don't like conflicts

    d) Do my best to control my anger but sometimes I just can't help showing how upset I feel

7. When I have to convince someone to do something, I:

    a) Wonder how I can excite them with my ideas

    b) Try to understand their underlying concerns

    c) Tell them what they should do

    d) Gather all the relevant information for a thorough presentation of the facts

8. When I have a problem, I:

    a) Ask for help from my co-workers

    b) Look for information on how similar problems have been dealt with in the past so I can determine the next logical steps

    c) Decide the direction I want to go in

    d) Try to come up with some creative new ideas

9. In a meeting I usually:

    a) Take charge

    b) Provide a little humor or fun

    c) Ask questions to make sure that the viewpoints of everyone are included

    d) Stick to the schedule to make sure we don't miss any details

10. If I don't get something I need to do my job, I:

    a) Develop creative ways to get things done

    b) Tell my boss exactly what I need and make sure I get it

    c) Give a detailed list to my boss of what I need, when I need it, and why I need it

    d) Do my best to get my work done even if I don't have everything I need

11. When my boss invites me out to lunch, I:

    a) Look forward to talking to my boss and getting to know her better

b) Stick to business topics

c) Think it will be fun

d) Prepare an update of the details and progress of my current projects to review

12. When someone makes a mistake, I:

a) Try to motivate them to do better next time

b) Try to make them feel better about it—after all everyone makes mistakes

c) Tell them

d) I carefully explain the details of the problem and take them step by step through the correct solution

13. I would consider quitting my current job if:

a) I wasn't promoted as quickly as I think I should be

b) The company forced me to make rush decisions without careful consideration of the facts

c) My boss didn't appreciate my creative contributions

d) I didn't get along with my co-workers

14. When I consider looking for a new job, I:

a) Call my friends and let them know that I'm looking—they know that I get bored after a while at a job so they're not surprised

b) Don't like to change jobs unless I absolutely have to

c) Carefully review my qualifications and compare them to information about other companies and jobs

d) Quickly call a placement agency—I don't like to waste time on jobs that may not be able to offer me what I'm worth

15. I prefer to communicate:

a) With brief e-mails or notes

b) In person—it's so much easier to convince someone in person

c) With carefully planned e-mails or messages that include all the relevant information and backup

d) In person—it's easier to listen to someone and get to know them in person

16. My work space is:
   a) Decorated with things that show high status or power
   b) Very neat with few distractions
   c) Comfortable—it has pictures of my family and friends
   d) Filled with fun pictures and items that reflect who I am

17. I prefer to dress in:
   a) Comfortable clothes
   b) Power suits
   c) Clothes that show my individuality
   d) A conservative and professional manner

18. When my boss doesn't notice I'm doing a good job, I:
   a) Hope she'll notice—I don't like to boast
   b) Let her know the great things I've done and the terrific things other people say about me
   c) Send her detailed proof of all the hard work that I have accomplished
   d) Tell her directly

19. I would describe myself as:
   a) Enthusiastic
   b) Friendly
   c) Logical
   d) Direct

20. I like to work with co-workers who are:
   a) Nice
   b) Results oriented
   c) Fun
   d) Detail oriented

After you score your assessment you should have a total number for each of the four areas: Bossy, Bubbly, Buddy, and Brainy.

Scoring

Directions: Circle your chosen answers. Count how many times you responded in each column and write the totals at the bottom of the columns.

Question Numbers				
1	D	C ✓	B	A
2	A	B	C	D ✓
3	A	C	B	D ✓
4	A	C	D	B ✓
5	D ✓	B	A	C
6	A	D	C	B ✓
7	C	A	D ✓	B
8	C	D	A	B ✓
9	A	B ✓	C	D ✓
10	B	A	D ✓	C
11	B	C	A	D ✓
12	C ✓	A	B	D
13	A	C	D	B ✓
14	D	A	B ✓	C
15	A	B	D	C ✓
16	A	D	C	B ✓
17	B	C	A	D ✓
18	D	B	A ✓	C
19	D	A	B	C ✓
20	B	C	A ✓	D
Total	2	2	5	12
	Bossy Type	**Bubbly Type**	**Buddy Type**	**Brainy Type**

Your highest score indicates which communication type you prefer to use at work. Your lowest score indicates which communication type you use least often or with which type you might have the biggest problems.

EXAMPLE

If your scores are:

Bossy — 10

Bubbly — 5

Brainy — 4

Buddy — 1

This would show that you typically talk the way a Bossy type does. This score also shows that you almost never deal with people the way a Buddy type would. You would probably find that you have the most problems when you deal with Buddy types because they act so differently from the way that you naturally do.

Now you're ready to learn about the 4 Bs.

FREQUENTLY ASKED QUESTIONS ABOUT THE QUIZ (FAQ)

I have two scores that are high. What does that mean?

If two of your scores are high, then you are comfortable with both communication types. Read both of the sections and decide what information describes you best.

I have three scores that are high. What does that mean?

If three of your scores are high, then you are comfortable in some ways with three communication types. Read all three of the sections and decide what information describes you best.

All of my scores are even, what should I do?

Review the quiz again. You may have made a mistake or you may be one of the lucky people who really are comfortable communicating with everyone. That is very unusual. I suggest that you read the chapters that describe all the different types and see which ones seem to be most like you.

I don't agree with my score.

I suggest that you thoroughly read the chapters that describe your high score. Some people don't like the labels that we use (Bossy, Bubbly, Buddy, Brainy); however, try to get beyond those words and look at the descriptions.

If you read the chapters that describe your high score and you still don't agree with it, then you should read all of the other chapters to see if the information on one of the other types matches you more closely. Remember, each section that describes a communication type is written to appeal to that type. The chapters that are easier for you to read are most likely chapters that describe your type and the chapters that are hard to read are most likely very different from you.

I've read the chapters and I agree with some of it but not all of it.

Of course not all of the information in the chapter will accurately describe you. You are an individual. The chapters will only give you general information. When you review the chapters, you should use what fits you. Keep the other information in mind even if you don't think that it describes you because it might help you to understand how other people deal with you.

I told my friends about my score and they don't agree.

What do you think? Your friends can help you to see yourself so you should consider their input; however, you know yourself best. Ask your friends to give you some specific information about why they think your score should be different. What did you say or what did you do that gave them that impression? They can give you some valuable feedback about how they see your actions. Read through the chapters with your high score and then read through the chapters with the communication type that they suggest. You may be comfortable with two communication types.

Or you may find out that the way you think is very different from your actions. For example, you might see yourself as a Buddy type (warm and friendly); however, when you communicate with others, you appear to be a Brainy type because you focus on step-by-step instructions and logical tasks, not feelings. It's important for you to understand why people see you in a different way.

Some people pick answers to the quiz that reflect how they would like to be, not the way they really deal with others. You may want to review your answers to see if that's how you really feel.

How do I get my co-worker to take the test so I can figure out what type she is?

It's very helpful to find out how your co-workers and your boss like to communicate. By understanding the people you work with, you can start to make small changes in the way you act so you can communicate better with them. That makes your job easier.

You may want to suggest that your co-workers take the test so you can compare scores. This is a great way to begin a productive discussion. You can talk about the ways you like to communicate and things you don't like. And your co-workers can help you to understand what works with them and what doesn't.

If you can't get your co-workers or boss to take the test, you can get an idea of their communication type by filling out the quiz in chapter 16 and answering questions about them. It won't be as accurate; however, it will give you some good information to help you to start to understand them better.

2   Understanding the 4Bs: Bossy, Bubbly, Buddy, Brainy

UNDERSTANDING THE 4B MODEL

The 4 B Model: Bossy, Bubbly, Buddy, and Brainy will help you to understand yourself better. It shows what you are comfortable doing and why others respond to you in certain ways. You can use this information to be more effective when dealing with others.

The model depicts the communication types as four overlapping circles. Each of the circles represents one of the types. The words outside the circles show the main descriptions.

4B Model

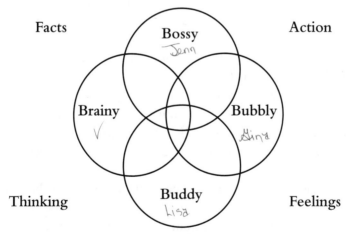

For example, Bossy types prefer to take Action and talk about Facts. They are direct and fast-paced. They like to confront problems as soon as they develop and don't let their personal feelings color their judgment. They say, "It's only business, it's nothing personal."

Bubbly types also like to take Action, but they talk about Feelings. Bubbly types smile and laugh much more than Bossy types and they like to spend time with other people. They are not afraid to share their feelings and may tell many personal stories — even to people they don't know well.

Buddy types, similar to Bubbly types, also like to talk about Feelings; however, they prefer to Think instead of taking Action. They like to consider information before they talk and tend to quietly share their concerns with others. They would prefer to subtly hint or suggest so they don't upset anyone else. They like to take time to really develop relationships and to get to know the people at work.

Brainy types also prefer Thinking instead of Action, but they differ from Buddy types because they talk about Facts when they communicate with others. They appear to be reserved and prefer to study problems before making suggestions. Brainy types don't want to talk about feelings and do not normally display emotions at work.

None of us exactly fits the descriptions of the communication types. We can't expect that four simple groupings will explain us entirely. Typically, however, there is one which is dominant, one with which we really identify. Sometimes, there is a secondary group that also seems to describe how we act. If you score high in several areas, then you are going to share characteristics of all those types.

Where the circles overlap is where you share some of the characteristics of others. Each person who fits a certain type is going to be different in some ways from others in the same type. Even though all Buddy types prefer Thinking and are concerned about Feelings, they don't all act in the same ways. Some Buddy types, for example, may share some characteristics of Brainy types and may communicate in a more structured and logical way. Or a

Buddy type may share some characteristics with Bubbly types, and may be more direct and faster to respond than a typical Buddy type.

For example, in the circles below, Michelle and Emma are both in the Buddy group, but there are some differences between them.

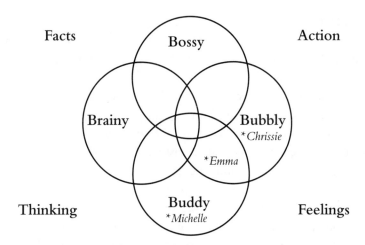

Michelle fits most of the characteristics that are typical for a Buddy type. She appreciates slower communication and really likes to get to know and understand people. Emma shares some characteristics that are normally associated with Bubbly types. She is faster paced and shows more enthusiasm than Michelle. Emma is a little more direct than Michelle when she talks to other people. When Michelle has a concern, she hints about it in a subtle way so she doesn't offend the other person. When Emma has a concern, instead of hinting at it, she mentions it outright.

Emma is not as direct as Chrissie, a Bubbly type. When Chrissie needs something, she lets you know right away and if she doesn't get it, then she continues to let you know. Emma doesn't feel comfortable being quite that bold. Emma fits the Buddy communication model and she also shares something in common with Bubbly types. When Emma reads the descriptions, she should focus mainly on the information about Buddy types but she should also review the information about the Bubbly group to find some suggestions that might help her.

APPRECIATING DIFFERENCES

The 4 Bs explain how people are most comfortable communicating. The model shows that different people do things in different ways and that's okay.

For example, let's say you're a Bubbly type working on a project. You may be very enthusiastic and want to brainstorm and quickly toss around some ideas. A Brainy type working on the same project may think that brainstorming is a total waste of time until she really understands the detailed requirements of the project. The Brainy type may want to study the information and make a list of what to do before discussing it with anyone else.

If you and the Brainy type are working together, you could have major disagreements if you don't understand each other. You could easily get impatient with her and she could think that you're dealing with the project in a very superficial way. If you both understand that you have your own ways of looking at the information and unique ways to work, then you can appreciate your differences.

That's the point. None of these approaches is wrong. They're just different. Once you realize that everyone is different, you can deal with people in a way that makes them at ease.

Each of the 4 Bs has its own special strengths and weaknesses. Your team at work will be most effective when you include people from each of these four types, since each one has a unique approach. In a highly effective group, a Bossy type will make sure that everyone stays focused on the bottom line and will move them forward, a Bubbly type will motivate the group and come up with new ideas, a Buddy type will make sure that everyone is involved and their feelings are considered and a Brainy type will take care of the details and make sure that nothing is missed. It's not easy to work in a group where everyone is so different; however, the results will be worth the effort. Without someone who is comfortable in each of these areas, your group will be missing something. So when you put together a team, try to make sure that you have representatives from each of the four communication types.

HANDLING SITUATIONS DIFFERENTLY

People who communicate differently handle the same situation in very different ways. For example, if you have four sales associates who must contact a difficult customer with a problem, each sales associate is going to react very differently. Imagine the customer wants to change an order and is going to be charged a penalty fee. Brenda, a Bossy type, is going to quickly and directly explain about the penalty and will let the customer know she'll take care of it right away. Bridget, a Bubbly type, may talk it over with her co-workers first to get ideas about how to deal with the customer. She's going to be extra friendly and may try to joke with the customer to lessen the tension. Betsy, a Buddy type, is going to worry about how the customer is going to feel about the charge. When she talks to the customer, she'll use her good listening skills to empathize and show that she understands the customer's concerns. Beverly, a Brainy type, is going to research past situations and be thoroughly ready with alternatives before contacting the customer. You can see that each of these women can be successful with the customer, but they each do it in a way in which they feel comfortable.

EVERYONE IS UNIQUE

Individual complexities can't be completely captured by a simple four-part model. Instead, the 4 B model should be used as a starting point to understand how others naturally communicate. When you understand the basics, you can begin to appreciate people as individuals so you can develop more positive relationships, whether at work or elsewhere.

You know that you are much more complex than your communication type and so are the people around you. For example, if you determine that a woman you work with is a Bossy type, that only gives you general information about how to start dealing with her. You still need to get to know her as a person to truly understand her.

NEXT STEPS

The next step is to read the section that describes you. Each section is written in a way that is easily understandable for a particular group. For example, the section for Bossy types, women who are Action-oriented and focused on Facts, is very short and to the point. The section for Bubbly types, women who are Action oriented and emphasize Feelings, includes more exciting and fun information. Each section begins with a chapter that describes the strengths of that group. The next chapter explains potential problems. The final chapter in each section gives you practical solutions for dealing with other people.

Then you'll want to read through the other chapters to understand the people around you. The more you understand them, the easier it will be for you to work with them. As you progress through the chapters, ask yourself which are easier for you to read and which are more difficult. The chapters that are hard for you to read probably represent people with whom you have the most problems.

If you're in a hurry, you can read the sections relevant to you and then and go right to the final chapters in the Becoming Successful section. This information will help you develop a plan of action to make changes.

Take charge of your career. Learn how people perceive you and do something about it now. Learn how the 4 B model can help you to be more successful.

II
The Bossy Type

3   Who is the Bossy Type?

WHAT ARE BOSSY TYPES LIKE?

It's all about results. You get things done. Some people may not like it but that's their problem. You don't have time or patience for people who can't keep up. It drives you crazy when people waste time with long-winded stories. Get to the point. Do it now. Get out of my way.

When you hear that people call you the dragon lady, you laugh. Hey, as long as you get your job done, it doesn't matter how you do it. This isn't a popularity contest. It's business. It's nothing personal.

You are:

- Results-oriented.
- Fast-paced.
- Assertive.
- A quick decision-maker.
- Time conscious.
- Direct and to the point.

RESULTS

When you're in charge, things get done. You're great at turning departments around. You like to be in command. You appear to be very professional, cool and confident.

Even when you're not in charge, you act like you are. You work hard to make sure that your results are noticed and you expect to be rewarded.

You make quick decisions. You don't have time for a lot of analysis. If you wait too long, you miss opportunities. You believe that even a bad decision is better than no decision. You think that taking risks is just part of the job. You are not afraid to disagree with other people's decisions and you're willing to fight for what you think is right.

     ☐   ☐   ☐   ☐   ☐   ☐   ☐   ☐   ☐

CASE STUDY # 1—DESCRIPTIONS

Debra (Bossy type)

Debra is an Operations Manager at work. She makes sure that product moves from the factories to customers around the world. Mistakes in her department can cause hundreds of thousand of dollars in lost revenue.

Debra is proud of the fact that since she took over the department two years ago, there have been no major problems. Before she got there, the department was often over budget and product shortages occurred regularly. She quickly straightened things out. Most of her new staff shaped up quickly, but two people who couldn't keep up were out.

She considers herself to be fair but firm with her staff—after all, she has a job to do.

WHAT SHE SAYS

Debra boasts that she has an open-door policy. She jokes, though, that she doesn't want her employees wasting her time with unnecessary nonsense. When she talks to employees she:
- Is fast-paced.
- Gets right to the point.
- Interrupts.
- Tells her opinion in a confident way.
- Openly disagrees with others when she thinks she is right.

WHAT SHE DOES

When employees come to her with problems, she quickly gets to the point. She makes fast decisions. When her staff does well, she praises them. If they make mistakes, she's just as quick to chew them out.

RESULTS

Debra says she gets great results and it's true. Her department has turned around since she took over. They consistently meet the product goals that Debra sets for them. When her employees do well, she makes sure they get rewarded and she fights with her boss and Human Resources to get bonuses for her staff.

Debra has received several promotions in a short time and she is well-known as someone who gets things done. She expects to be promoted to Director soon.

4   Bossy Problems

WHAT'S THE PROBLEM?

If you're a Bossy type, you focus on getting things done, not on people's feelings. People don't always like that. Here are things you do that cause problems with others:

You:

- Openly criticize people (sometimes in front of others) when they don't meet your high standards.
- Appear unconcerned about people's personal lives.
- Don't consider people's feelings when you talk to them.
- Don't often smile – so people think you're mad.
- Directly challenge people when you don't agree.
- Make quick decisions with limited information and little input from others.
- Are confident that you are right and do not need to listen to opinions of others.
- Overcome obstacles by crushing them.
- Don't waste time on activities that you think don't obviously connect to business results, such as office parties.
- Address problems directly without adding niceties that could soften the message.

You see these behaviors as assertive. You're just trying to get things done. Someone's got to take charge. Other people may see your behavior as aggressive and attacking. You think of business as war. There are winners and losers. You're one of the winners.

SO WHAT?

People who are not like you tend to avoid you. And that's fine with you. If they can't handle it, then you don't want to waste your time with them. Unfortunately, other people can cause big problems for you.

PROBLEMS WITH EMPLOYEES

- Employees are afraid to make decisions because they're afraid that you won't agree.
- Employees won't give you bad news because they don't want to be chewed out, so you're unaware of important problems until it's too late.
- Employees are reluctant to challenge you or to ask questions, so mistakes are made.
- Angry employees sabotage projects to get back at you.
- Employees do only what you ask them to do and nothing more.
- Employees avoid you, if at all possible.
- Employees lack loyalty and quit with little or no notice.

PROBLEMS WITH PEERS

- Peers avoid speaking to you about things that may cause disagreements so you are left out of the loop.
- Peers don't invite you to events because they don't enjoy your company so you miss out on valuable networking opportunities.

PROBLEMS WITH YOUR BOSS
AND UPPER MANAGEMENT

- You miss out on assignments that require tact and diplomacy.
- You are overlooked for promotions that require someone with excellent communication skills.
- You are not invited to vital meetings because they are afraid that you're going to start an argument.

You think other people should lead, follow or get out of the way. And most often they should just get out of your way and let you do your work the way it needs to be done. You need to modify your approach, unless you plan to do everything yourself. If people don't want to work with you it will make it harder to get things done. You need better communication skills so people will trust you and will want to work with you.

The bottom line is that if you don't learn how to communicate with others in ways that make them comfortable, you will be limited in how high you can move up in the company. Learn how to communicate better and you can be much more successful.

□ □ □ □ □ □ □ □

CASE STUDY #1 — ISSUES

Debra (Bossy type)

Debra, the Operations Manager, has high turnover in her department, but she doesn't mind because if people can't keep up then she doesn't have time for them. Debra says that the Human Resources group hires unqualified people for her area. Human Resources say she is too picky and difficult to work with.

Debra's Administrative Assistant, Emma, does a good job but drives Debra crazy. Emma never seems to get to the point and can't make a decision by herself. Debra prides herself on having an open door policy; however, she can't waste her time answering every stupid question that her employees have. Isn't that why she pays them?

Emma is looking for another job and is going to quit as soon as she finds something else. She wants to work in a friendlier environment where she can ask questions without getting a sarcastic response.

Debra is well known around the office for her caustic comments and her hard-driving manner. She dismisses this criticism as jealousy by some of her peers who are not as successful as she is. She gets results when it counts.

Kate, in the Shipping Department, complains that Debra doesn't pay attention to details and some of her deadlines are unrealistic. Kate is tired of arguing with Debra and often tries to deal directly with her employees instead. Kate decided not to bother to give Debra information about future schedule problems since she doesn't seem to listen.

Debra has made it clear that she is interested in a promotion. Her group has met and exceeded all production goals. Debra's boss, Stephanie, says she is pleased with the results.

Stephanie appreciates Debra's direct manner; however, she has suggested that a friendlier approach might work better. She wants Debra to spend more time motivating her employees.

Stephanie doesn't think that Debra has what it takes to be a Director yet. Debra gets things done, but manages to pulverize everything in her way. Directors need to get results without alienating people.

5   Taming the Bossy Type

WHAT NOW?

As a Bossy type, you need to realize the effect you have on other people. Then you can make some minor adjustments to get better results.

WORKING WITH ANOTHER BOSSY TYPE

If you agree on where you're going, it can be great to work with someone like you. You both like to take Action and prefer to talk about Facts instead of Feelings. You don't waste time with chitchat and you can trust her to get the results you need.

But if you don't agree on the direction, watch out! Since you're both convinced that you can do it best, you may want to divide the project so you can each take control of a separate part. If you can't split up the project, you may have to back off a little, especially if the other person is your boss.

WORKING WITH A BUBBLY TYPE

Bossy types and Bubbly types are both Action-oriented and direct. However, Bubbly types show their emotions where Bossy types are emotionally reserved.

The bottom line is that working with a Bubbly type is going to take longer than you want. When you get together, schedule extra time so you can hear her ideas and brainstorm with her. It seems like a waste of time. You don't have to like it; just do it. You'll get better results. Also, plan to spend 5 minutes asking about her hobbies or activities outside of work before you get to business. That will make it easier to work with her.

If you want to convince a Bubbly type to agree to a new commission plan for salespeople, you need to get her excited about it. Talk about how it will motivate people and get them to do their best. Ask for her creative suggestions about how to sell it to employees. Support her ideas for a big kick-off meeting that will add excitement.

WORKING WITH A BUDDY TYPE

Buddy types are the communication group most different from you. Buddy types have a Thinking orientation and they like to talk about Feelings. These are the people you're going to have the most problems with. You consider them to be too slow. They hint about things and never seem to get to the point. They spend their time talking about personal issues rather than focusing on work.

Your natural reaction is to either avoid them or steamroll right over them to get what you want. It seems to work well for you in the short term; however, it can cause resistant employees and passive-aggressive behavior. If you need to work with a Buddy type, you're going to have to develop a relationship with her.

Schedule plenty of time, even more time than with a Bubbly type. You need to get to know a Buddy type personally, before she'll be comfortable working with you. Ask about her family and activities outside of work.

Buddy types don't like to be direct since it can lead to disagreements. To get information, you'll have to question her in a friendly manner. Ask open-ended questions that require more than a "yes" or "no" answer. Example of good open-ended questions to use would be: "How was your weekend?" or "What do you think of the new sales plan?" Don't use close-ended questions such as: "Did you go away last weekend?" or "Don't you think the new sales plan is a good idea?" It may seem like a waste of time, trying to pull the information out of her, however, she's just not comfortable volunteering. You need to ask.

Really listen to her without interrupting even if she's talking about things you don't care about. Don't try to finish her sentences for her to hurry her along. Buddy types really want to know that they are being listened to. And if they don't feel listened to—they may talk even more to get you to listen. So stop interrupting ad just let them talk.

If you're trying to get a Buddy type to agree to a new sales commission plan, you need to include information about personal concerns. Find out what people think about the plan and how it will affect them. Don't talk about what the plan will do for the company; you'll need to show how it will benefit individuals. Explain that with the new sales commission plan, Lucy, in the accounting department, can earn more money so she can buy that house she's been mentioning.

Listen to the Buddy type's concerns and show her how happy the employees will be with the plan. If you have already built a relationship with her and she trusts you, she will be more likely to agree with you.

WORKING WITH A BRAINY TYPE

Bossy types and Brainy types both focus on Facts so you don't have to talk about Feelings. Unfortunately for you, Brainy types prefer Thinking over Action. They don't get to the point. They spend too much time reviewing unnecessary information in your opinion. They value details and procedures and have difficulty talking about the big picture.

Your natural inclination is to push them to go faster, but you're going to have to schedule additional time to work with a Brainy type to discuss details and specific procedures. If you try to go faster, they'll just avoid you or slow down even more.

If you're trying to persuade a Brainy type that you should have a new sales commission plan, you need to use facts. Let her know what has been done in the past and what the results were. Explain why you are considering a new plan and what research you have done. Show the effect on sales and explain, in detail, how the process will work. Work out all the possible numbers and include charts and graphs. All the questions need to be answered before the Brainy type will begin to consider making a change.

CHECKLIST

Bossy type
> ✓Decide who's in charge.
> ✓Do it.

Bubbly type
> ✓Ask about her interests.
> ✓Share her enthusiasm.

Buddy type
> ✓Slow down.
> ✓Don't interrupt.
> ✓Draw out information by using open-ended questions.
> ✓Listen.

Brainy type
> ✓Provide numbers and details.
> ✓Give historical information.
> ✓Explain processes and procedures thoroughly.

❑ ❑ ❑ ❑ ❑ ❑ ❑ ❑

CASE STUDY #1 — SOLUTIONS

Debra (Bossy type)

After Debra learned about the 4B model, she realized that she came across as negative to some of the people at work. She blocked out time to spend with her Administrative Assistant, Emma, whom she decided was a Buddy type. When Emma made a mistake, rather than blowing up, Debra asked Emma what she could learn from it.

Emma was shocked. She had expected the usual sarcastic response. Emma decided to stay at her job and worked even harder to understand what Debra needed. The rest of the staff noticed the changes in Debra. She still had high standards; however, rather than yell at people who couldn't reach her standards, she coached them to do better. People worked even harder, not out of fear, but out of respect for her.

The next time that Kate asked for shipping information for her department, Debra dealt with her differently. Debra decided that Kate was a Brainy type and gave her the specific information that she needed and patiently answered her questions.

Kate was relieved. Debra wasn't so hard to deal with after all. Kate provided additional information to Debra on possible scheduling conflicts that could help her to avoid costly mistakes.

Debra decided to soften her approach with Stephanie, her boss, a Bubbly type. Debra asked for advice on how to motivate her employees. She smiled more and made time for jokes and small talk.

Stephanie was pleased at Debra's increased friendliness. It seemed to her that Debra was finally figuring out that you can't run a successful department on numbers alone. Stephanie could feel the difference in Debra's department when she went to visit.

People seemed more committed, more relaxed, and more excited about working for Debra.

Debra realized that in order to get promoted she must convince the executives that she could handle people. She asked Stephanie to assign her to a committee where she would have the opportunity to work with some of the executives and display her new communication skills. She also worked on her relationships with colleagues and scheduled time to make sure she talked to them in a friendly and casual manner.

Stephanie talked to the executives about promoting Debra to take over a larger department. They haven't agreed, but they have said that Debra is going in the right direction. They still need more time to make sure that the changes aren't only temporary.

III
The Bubbly Type

6   Who is the Bubbly Type?

You want work to be fun! If it isn't fun, you need to do something about it – have a party, go out for pizza or have a silly photo contest. After all, we spend so much time at work; we might as well enjoy it. Right? ☺

DEALING WITH OTHERS

You're enthusiastic and you like to work with other fun people! You laugh easily and try to get other people to laugh too. After all, didn't they do some study on that? You know, it takes fewer muscles to smile than to frown. You absolutely believe that. People around you comment that you smile often and always seem to be in a good mood. Smiling is contagious and you're hoping that everyone around catches it!

Let's talk about other people—without them, the job would be dull, dull, dull! You can't understand anyone who likes to work alone. ☹ You couldn't do it. You need human interaction every day. And if you do have to work by yourself, you make sure that you often step out of your office to talk with people or call people to get ideas. Actually, you do your best work when you're talking to other people. Ideas just seem to tumble out of your mouth when you talk to others. You'd much rather spend time with people than sit by yourself doing research.

You *really* like to talk. Typically, you're among the first to jump in with ideas when people ask for suggestions. You're not shy about voicing your opinions and you enjoy bantering with others about many different topics. And you don't mind quickly jumping from one idea to another. You like multitasking and are good at doing several things at once.

People who talk too slowly drive you crazy. When you have to wait for other people, you don't like it. If only people could pick up the pace a little bit, it would make things much easier.

You also have problems with people who don't have good attitudes. "Don't worry. Be happy!" That's you! And if you're around grumpy people, you do your best to cheer them up, whether they want your help or not.

You work hard to make sure that people around you are happy. ☺ You're at your best when you are motivating people, cheering them on, getting them to do even more than they had expected. You're fun to have around! You suggest holding birthday parties and baby showers. Other people may do the actual planning but you're always ready to add some creative ideas.

You like networking games at meetings and parties and think it's great to meet new people. You're energetic and like to get people moving around. You're the queen of networking and know many people in different areas.

PLANNING

You're fast-paced. You don't like to wait and you'd rather just jump in and do something than spend too much time on evaluation. You figure that some action is better than no action. "Ready, Fire, Aim," sometimes describes the way you approach your job. If you make a mistake, you know that you can always fix it somehow. Of course you do plan, but sometimes you have to take action instead of spending months evaluating possibilities.

You're terrific at seeing the big picture. You can easily create a vision of where you want your group to go. You can paint pictures with your words. People see you as a leader whether you have the title or not. That's fine with you, since you enjoy being the center of attention. ☺ You like public recognition.

OVERVIEW

Excitement! New challenges! That's what gets you going! You can't imagine doing the same old stuff every day. That's why you thrive on jobs that have a lot of change or uncertainty in them. You get bored easily and may be ready to leave jobs after a few months unless they keep your interest.

People like to be around you and tell you how fun you are. It's easy for you to get a group of people together and motivate them. It comes naturally to you. People love working with and for you! ☺ You make sure that everyone has a good time and gets the job done.

You easily come up with creative ideas and fresh solutions. You aren't tied to the past and you believe there's always room for improvement. You like looking at the big picture and can help other people share your visions.

You get things done! And you're great at launching other people into action! You get the ball rolling!

        ▫ ▫ ▫ ▫ ▫ ▫ ▫ ▫ ▫

CASE STUDY #2 — DESCRIPTION

Chrissie (Bubbly type)

Chrissie is a Human Resources Supervisor. Her real name is Christine, but no one ever calls her that. She loves the excitement of her job. ☺ She never knows what's going to happen each day. She enjoys it when people come to her to talk things over.

She's only been at her job for a few months, but she's already put in some great new programs to add some life to the company. She started the first Summer Outing to get the employees together. She also instituted a Suggestion Box to find out what was bothering employees. And the training programs that she started on Communication Skills have been a real hit.

WHAT SHE SAYS

Chrissie speaks enthusiastically about new ideas and likes to brainstorm in meetings. She tells stories to illustrate her points and often adds colorful details. She doesn't talk about problems; she instead calls them challenges and tries to see the positive side of every situation. She feels that talking can solve most issues. She prefers to discuss situations in person rather than send an e-mail or leave a voicemail. It's just more personal.

WHAT SHE DOES

Chrissie comes to work every day with a smile on her face. She is serious about doing a good job; however, she feels that she must present a positive image to keep the employees motivated. Even if she isn't feeling well, she says to herself that "the show must go on" and it's up to her to look happy and enthusiastic.

When she talks, she uses hand gestures and facial expressions to make points. She looks energetic and she likes to keep moving. She laughs easily.

She makes sure that other people feel good and she asks how they are doing. She wants the company to be a fun place to work. She wants people to enjoy their jobs and to look forward to coming to work.

RESULTS

The people who work with Chrissie like being part of her team. They're enthusiastic and appreciate the praise that Chrissie gives them when they do a good job. And when things don't go smoothly, they're glad that Chrissie can see the bright side. As a result, her employees work hard and have fun.

7   Bubbly Problems

PROBLEMS? WHAT PROBLEMS?

You're so much fun to be with, how can there be problems? ☺
Unfortunately, not everyone enjoys working with you. And there
are some major problems that you may experience at work.

PLANNING AND DETAILS

You're a big picture person! You have grand ideas! You don't like
to get bogged down in little details. You think that's a waste of
your talent. Of course you don't mind dealing with a few details,
but for a big project, you'd rather have someone else handle all the
minor points. Unfortunately, your lack of attention to detail may
make you miss important information.

You tend to avoid detailed analysis, because you think it takes
too long. You'd rather rely on your gut instincts. Sometimes your
gut is right, but not always. And it's hard to explain to upper management the reasons for your choices when something, "just felt
like the right thing to do." They want hard data and numbers.
Critical and strategic thinkers are the ones who continue to move
up, not people who jump into things and think about it later.

As for planning, you think that's very overrated. ☺You like to do
things on the fly, with little preparation. You think you work well
under pressure and are great at quick responses. Of course you do
spend some time planning; however, you're much more comfortable when you quickly assess something and jump right in. That
approach can be good for small decisions, but when company
money is at stake, you need to spend more time planning. In addition, your reluctance to plan drives some of your co-workers

crazy. You know the ones. They have charts and graphs and want to spend months evaluating possibilities. They're so difficult to work with!

ORGANIZATION AND TIME MANAGEMENT

Time management is a real struggle for you. ☺☹ You thrive on change and flexibility. That means even if you do put together a schedule for yourself, you don't feel the need to follow it. A schedule feels so restrictive!! After all, how can you plan for all the things that come up? You want to have the freedom to spend time working with people rather than worrying about opening your mail at 9:30. That causes problems when people expect you to follow schedules and you often find yourself running late for meetings.

Getting organized is hard for you. Your desk may look like a hurricane blew through leaving piles of papers. You swear that you know where everything is; however, you end up wasting time trying to look for things. Part of the reason that you have so much junk on you desk is because you tend to jump from one project to another. You thrive on jobs where you are working on many projects at one time. Unfortunately you don't often have time to finish the paperwork from one project before you remember that you have to work on another project.

And regarding paperwork – UGH! You would rather do any-thing than paperwork. You resent the time you have to spend filling out reports and forms – that's time you could be spending with other people. Paperwork is often delayed until you can't put it off any longer.

SHOWING EMOTIONS

Okay, so sometimes you get a little overly dramatic. ☺ When you tell stories, you make them exciting and entertaining. You can make a simple story of going to the post office sound like an epic struggle. You tend to be the center of attention. Other people may not appreciate this and they may resent the attention that you get. And not everyone enjoys your embellishments and dramatic stories. Sometimes they just want the facts.

It's hard for you to disguise your emotions. When you're happy, you show it. You do not have a poker face. People can easily read your emotions and that can put you at a disadvantage at work when negotiating with others.

When you're mad, it's hard to hide it. Your face says it all. Employees know to keep away from you when you're in a bad mood. After you get angry, you feel much better and it's over for you. You are comfortable moving quickly from one emotion to another. However, you don't realize that your colleagues may hold onto grudges long after you've forgotten about them.

OVERSTATING

You're good at over-promising. You don't mean to. When you promise something you're sure you can find some way to make it work. You just don't know how yet. Unfortunately, you can't always figure things out in time. So you end up promising customers and employees things that you don't deliver. This is a reputation that can very quickly hurt you. If people expect that you over-promise or over-inflate the information you give out, they will be reluctant to believe anything you say.

FOCUS ON FUN

You're so busy trying to keep other people motivated that you don't realize your job is not company cheerleader. You feel you have to put on a good show every day. You think people depend on you to create a happy mood. That's not necessarily what people want. They don't want someone with rose-colored glasses always telling them that everything's going to work out in the end. They want someone who's going to realistically assess the situation and deal with it. You are not responsible for cheering up everyone else.

When you act cheerful all the time, people don't take you seriously. They see your playful and fun side and don't realize that you have a more serious side. Of course you keep that side hidden – in some cases well hidden. That's why you may get the reputation of being a party animal or the office clown. That's going to hurt you when they need someone serious to do a job.

SHORT ATTENTION SPAN

Excitement! New challenges! That's what gets you going! You can't imagine doing the same old stuff every day. You like to jump from one project to another and you have a hard time finishing things up before going on to something new and interesting. Sometimes this means that you procrastinate on things you think are dull or boring. You just never seem to find time to get around to them.

You thrive on jobs that have lots of change or uncertainty. You get bored easily and may be ready to switch jobs after a few months unless they keep your interest. The idea of staying at one job for 30 years is repulsive!!! You wonder how anyone could do that. Your resume may show many changes, not only job changes but also you may change industries and professions. You want to try new things and don't like to be restricted by what other people think are good career moves.

When you quickly move from one thing to another, you lose the opportunity to dig deeper into different areas. You may get superficial knowledge about many jobs but don't take the time to specialize. Employers do not want to see resumes that show a lot of random jumping around. They want to see reasonable progression. After all, why should they hire you, if you're probably going to get bored quickly and quit.

TALKING TOO MUCH AND INTERRUPTING

When you're with other people, do you dominate the conversation? Of course you do! You have so much to say! Are quiet people bowled over by how much you talk? Bubbly types often talk too much and too fast. It's hard for slower people to get in and make a point. You have no problem interrupting others. Listen to yourself in conversations. Do you often finish people's sentences for them? That is a habit that can really annoy others and can restrict the information they give you.

You may find that you especially interrupt people who talk slowly. They... go... so... slow!!! ☹ Argghh! It's so annoying. If only they'd speed up, it'd be much easier. So you interrupt them and try to get them to pick up the pace a little bit. And if there's a pause in the conversation, you fill it with your witty remarks. You're not comfortable with holes in the conversation – you think there should be constant talking. You don't realize that some people want pauses in the conversation. That gives them the opportunity to think and to respond.

You need to talk in order to think. So you may not think before you speak. Words just seem to tumble out of your mouth. And your spontaneity causes problems. There have been plenty of times when you wished that you could put a brake on your tongue before it said something else that would get you into trouble. If you're known as someone who isn't careful about what you say, you won't be assigned to projects with delicate implications. Your bosses will be afraid that you'll blurt out information that shouldn't be shared.

You like to talk about your personal life, and I do mean personal. You may share intimate details about yourself and your family that other people may not be quite comfortable sharing. And in some cases, they're not comfortable hearing the information from you. When you share very personal details about your life, your boss and colleagues wonder if you will be able to keep company secrets. They may be reluctant to give you access to confidential information, such as raises, for fear that you'll tell it to other people.

When you talk, you use a lot of gestures and facial expressions to get your points across. You become very animated. The tone of your voice contains a lot of information. Whether your voice is dripping with sarcasm or showing excitement, the way you say something is very expressive.

In your written communication, you often use a lot of exclamation points!! You may also use smiling faces or winking faces to show emotions. ☺ Your communication tends to include lots of motivational information and stories about people. It may not include a lot of hard data to back it up. That can irritate people who want their communication to be impersonal and to the point.

SO WHAT DO YOU DO?

If you want to be known as the Company Clown or Group Cheerleader, you don't need to do anything. If you are hoping to be seen as a leader of your organization, you need to make some changes in the way you approach people. You know that you're smart and capable, but the way you present yourself may undermine your message and cause problems for you at work.

Turn to the next chapter to see what you can do to be taken seriously at work while still enjoying yourself.

☐ ☐ ☐ ☐ ☐ ☐ ☐ ☐

CASE STUDY # 2 — ISSUES

Chrissie (Bubbly type)

Chrissie, the Human Resources Supervisor, is frustrated by how long everything seems to take. Why don't the senior managers want to do new things?

When Chrissie suggested offering every other Friday afternoon off in the summer, she met a lot of resistance. The executives said that they'd never done anything like it and wanted details on how it would affect productivity. It was frustrating because she didn't have hard numbers on productivity increases, but she knew it would really make a difference to the employees. It would help retention and increase morale. Why couldn't they see that?

When Chrissie gave a presentation on her idea to let employees take every other Friday afternoon off, Fran, the Finance Director, couldn't believe it. There were no facts to back up her proposal and only a vague cost analysis on the impact to the company. Fran said that she would review it when the executive group was given a thorough analysis. Fran figured that Chrissie would not bother with the analysis and would just jump to some other new idea.

Chrissie has also had problems with Kim, one of the section supervisors. Kim was unhappy because Chrissie hadn't hired enough people for her section. Chrissie had tried to talk to her about it but Kim seemed to be very vague about what she wanted. Chrissie jumped in with suggestions but none of them seemed to be right for Kim.

Kim wished that Chrissie would stop trying to push her for answers. Kim felt overwhelmed when Chrissie talked to her. Chrissie talked quickly and didn't seem to listen to what Kim was trying to say.

Chrissie is also having some problems with her boss, Anna.

Chrissie introduced a newsletter to let people know what's going on in the company. Anna did not share Chrissie's enthusiasm and said that Chrissie should spend her time addressing the problems with the salary program. Chrissie has been putting it off and said she'd get to it as soon as she could.

Anna thinks the newsletter is a waste of time and has clearly told Chrissie to focus on the salary program. Chrissie says she is too busy to start working on the salary program even though she seems to have plenty of time to spend on fun but non-essential projects. Anna is beginning to wonder if Chrissie can handle the more serious parts of the job.

Chrissie wants to move up in the organization, but Anna says she's not ready. Chrissie feels that she is ready and thinks that some of the upper level managers are too resistant to change. She has some great ideas and she wishes they would listen to her and agree with her suggestions.

Anna wants to see Chrissie prove that she can focus on the important aspects of the job before she considers promoting her.

Chrissie wonders if her hard work is worth it. She's considering looking for another job with a company that really wants to make a difference with its employees.

8   Making the Bubbly Type Serious

WORKING WITH OTHER TYPES

The great news is that you can make some minor changes to the way you communicate and you can get along much better with people. Let's take a look at what you can do right away to have more fun at work!

WORKING WITH A BOSSY TYPE

There are times you don't mind working with Bossy types. After all, you appreciate their fast-paced approach to the job. Other times though, they really seem like ice princesses. They are cold and frosty and you see yourself as much warmer. They don't laugh at your jokes and they're just a little too hard-edged.

So, what do you do when you have to work with a Bossy type? Fortunately, you can capitalize on the traits you both share. You are both Action oriented and willing to jump right in and get things done. You both dislike details and want to focus on the big picture. You're both fast-paced and tend to interrupt each other.

Where the two of you differ is how you express emotions. Bossy types tend to focus on Facts and come across as emotionally reserved. You focus on Feelings and like to demonstrate your emotions. Your face clearly shows how you are feeling, while a Bossy type has a poker face. You want to get to know the people whom you work with and have a little fun with them. Bossy types want to get the job done right away and don't like to take time for things you think are important.

When you work with a Bossy type, you need to remember that she doesn't like to waste time, and she doesn't like to spend time on personal matters. Don't ask her how her weekend was or try to discuss your personal plans. You need to get right to the point. If a Bossy type asks about your weekend, that's not an invitation to tell her all about your Aunt Martha's 75th birthday party, complete with balloons and a DJ and how Uncle Vern flew all the way in from Seattle to surprise everyone. The correct response is brief, such as, "Great weekend; I went to a family party. How was yours?" That might even be more information than the Bossy type wants, but it's acceptable.

When you're trying to persuade a Bossy type to do something, don't use stories to support your position. Use facts. For example, if you're trying to get a Bossy type to subsidize employee participation in a local gym, don't talk about how much the employees will like it and how happy they will be. And certainly, don't go on and on about how it will increase motivation. That will turn her off entirely.

Instead, briefly state the facts, such as how participation will reduce the amount the company spends on medical costs. That's it. You should have all the numbers prepared, but a quick summary or executive overview is all that a Bossy type wants.

One of the biggest problems that Bubbly types have when they try to persuade a Bossy type is overselling. Bossy types don't need to share your excitement. They just want to know that it makes sense.

WORKING WITH ANOTHER BUBBLY TYPE

It's great working with someone like you. ☺ The two of you really seem to click and end up finishing each other's sentences. You think it would be great if everyone else could act like this. Another Bubbly type can share your enthusiasm and excitement. She'll love to brainstorm and come up with creative and innovative solutions.

Unfortunately, two Bubbly types can also go too far and get outrageous. You can waste time having too much fun.

When you work with another Bubbly type, enjoy it! Just make sure that you are actually accomplishing whatever you're supposed to do by the deadline. If you're spending too much time having fun, then you need to keep refocusing on the task. If you come up with ideas that are too creative, you need to push back for more practical solutions. Use the energy that you get from working together, like two sparklers that make each other brighter. Just make sure that you focus on what you need to deliver, and push the other Bubbly type to do the same.

WORKING WITH A BUDDY TYPE

Buddy types are so nice that at first you think working with them will be easy. Then you realize that Buddy types work sooooo slowly. It's hard for you to slow down. And while you enjoy the camaraderie, there are times that you just want to take the project and run with it so it can be completed. Buddy types and Bubbly types both focus on Feelings, but they do it in different ways. Bubbly types tend to show their emotions in a very obvious way and Buddy types are much more guarded and subtle about their emotions. When a Bubbly type has something to say, she says it. When a Buddy type has something to say, she may wait until she is asked or someone draws it out of her. This can cause problems for Bubbly types who are not used to digging for emotions.

With Buddy types, you need to be aware of their emotions so if they get quiet, you need to ask them why. Unfortunately, Bubbly types tend to be so noisy that they might not notice how quiet the other person is. They may just assume that if the other person has something to say, she would say it.

You also need to be careful about hurting a Buddy type's feelings. Your upfront and direct style means that you say things sometimes without thinking about them. Buddy types tend to be sensitive and will not normally tell you if you have offended them, unless you have pushed them too far. You need to be aware of subtle clues, such as extended silence or people avoiding you. If that happens, it is best to take the time to ask the Buddy type what is wrong. You may need to ask a few times because some Buddy types will not want to tell you right away unless they are sure you really want to know. And when she does tell you, you need to listen without interrupting.

If you are trying to persuade a Buddy type to subsidize gym membership for employees, you would want to focus on the personal impact it would make on people. For example, you might talk about how Sally in Marketing said that she'd really like to lose those extra pounds that she gained when she was pregnant. And mention Carl in Engineering, and how he had to give up skiing because of his bad knees, but would still like to stay in shape. You would then discuss how happy it would make them. And you may also point out how hard they work and how much they deserve a break. A Buddy type will respond to concerns about other people.

One big mistake that Bubbly types make with Buddy types is interrupting them. Buddy types tend to speak more slowly and leave pauses in the conversation. Bubbly types are uncomfortable with silence and see these pauses as opportunities to jump in with more information. Instead, Bubbly types need to slow down and stop talking. This gives Buddy types the opportunity to share information.

Bubbly types also need to learn to ask open-ended questions of Buddy types and wait for the answers. An example of a good question is, "What do you think about that?" Or you can ask, "How will the employees react to this?" Bubbly types tend to like to tell people their opinions. If you do ask questions, it's normally to get people to answer in a certain way to guide them to agree with you. And Bubbly types have a hard time waiting for the answers. Give the Buddy types time. They need time to think. They need time to answer. They need pauses to consider if there is any other information they should add. And Bubbly types have to learn not to interrupt and to keep quiet. In some cases, you may actually have to force yourself to keep you mouth shut and bite your tongue if you have a habit of saying things when you shouldn't.

WORKING WITH A BRAINY TYPE

These are the hardest people with whom you will work. The way they communicate is the opposite of how you're comfortable. And they just drive you crazy. They take way too long to do anything, focus on boring little details, and are no fun at all. Imagine the effect that you have on them. They think you are loud, self-centered and superficial. So how do you work together?

One way to make communication easier with a Brainy type is to slow down. Like the Buddy type, a Brainy type normally spends more time processing information than you do. They are not as spontaneous as you are. So when you need an answer from a Brainy type, don't expect her to be able to give you one on the spot. Ask her a question and then give her some time to think about it and get back to you.

You may have to slow down your speech and put more pauses in the conversations, similar to what you do when you're talking to Buddy types. Another simple thing that you can do that will make a huge difference in the way you communicate is to stop interrupting. It's not easy, but if you do nothing more than stop interrupting a Brainy type, communication will be much improved. She needs pauses in the conversation. Resist the urge to jump in and finish sentences for her or prod her to finish a thought. Remember, Brainy types need time to think before they talk. You're used to thinking at the same time you're talking or sometimes talking before you think.☺

Another thing you can do that will make a big difference to a Brainy type is to organize your information in a logical manner. For example, if you are trying to persuade a Brainy type to subsidize a gym membership for your employees, you should first get all the facts and details, including things like actual cost per person, the amount that the company would pay and expected reduction in medical premiums. Then you would get supporting and historical data. For example, you would get information from other companies that had already done this so you could compare their expected savings to their actual savings. And if you could get this information for several previous years, that would be best. But you might be thinking, this is way too much information. And it's very boring! It wouldn't sell me. Of course, it wouldn't sell you, but you're not a Brainy type. A Brainy type needs that kind of information in order to make a decision.

It's not easy, but you can do it! By making some simple changes in the way you approach the people you work with, you can motivate others and have more fun! So go for it! ☺

QUICK CHECKLIST FOR DEALING WITH DIFFERENT TYPES

For the Bossy type:
    ✓Don't show excitement.
    ✓Keep information brief and to the point.

For the Bubbly Type:
    ✓Have fun, but don't forget to focus on the job.
    ✓Share her creativity and enthusiasm.

For the Buddy type:

✓Slow down your conversation by speaking carefully and stopping completely when you are done with a thought so she has time to comment.

✓Don't just focus on you and how you feel about a topic. Ask her open-ended questions (questions that can't be answered with "yes" or "no") to draw out how she feels about the discussion.

✓Be careful about hurting her feelings.

For the Brainy type:

✓Stop talking so much. Allow silences in the conversation.

✓Speak methodically and don't interrupt her, no matter how s-l-o-w-l-y she speaks.

✓Focus on facts not emotions and include as many number and statistics as possible to support your ideas.

✓Don't surprise a Brainy type with information. Give her time to think about something before she responds to you.

✓Send her information before meetings.

✓Be prepared with historical data. You need to let her know previous results.

◻ ◻ ◻ ◻ ◻ ◻ ◻ ◻

CASE STUDY # 2 — SOLUTIONS

Chrissie (Bubbly type)

Chrissie, the Human Resources Supervisor, learned about the 4 Bs and discussed it with some of her friends. She decided to use her new knowledge to communicate better with the people at her company.

Chrissie tried a new approach with Fran, the Finance Director.

She decided that Fran was a Brainy type. Instead of giving Fran a colorful computer presentation, Chrissie sent her a report with a careful analysis of the issues. After Fran had time to review it, Chrissie met with her and calmly discussed the facts. Chrissie slowed down and controlled her emotions by reminding herself to keep a poker face. There were times when she wanted to interrupt and jump in with ideas; however, she bit her tongue and waited.

Fran was impressed with the changes that Chrissie made in her presentation. When Chrissie presented the plan for a new medical insurance program, she included maximum and minimum costs. She gave background information and detailed medical costs for the past 5 years. She also showed specific numbers provided by a respected consulting company detailing what other companies were doing to reduce the rising medical insurance costs. It was almost all of the information that Fran needed. She was relieved that Chrissie did not get emotional. Fran noticed that Chrissie didn't seem as agitated as usual and had stopped making annoying little jokes. Fran decided that she would seriously consider the proposal.

When Chrissie dealt with Kim (a Buddy type) she tried to slow down and stop interrupting. Chrissie asked Kim for her suggestions and waited while she answered.

Kim was relieved that Chrissie had finally calmed down. Kim felt that Chrissie was quite pleasant to talk to when she was not so pushy.

Chrissie realized that her boss, Anna, was a Bossy type. Chrissie decided that she needed to take action on projects that Anna thought were important. Chrissie made sure that she did not waste Anna's time and gave her quick answers. She also tried to use less emotion in her discussions with Anna.

Anna was pleased that Chrissie was beginning to focus on the more important parts of the job. Chrissie really seemed to be learning.

Chrissie considered what she could gain from leaving the company. She decided that she still had a lot to learn and knew that her resume would look better if she stayed longer. That would also give her more time to really develop a specialty. She knew she could find ways to get along with everyone while still enjoying herself.

IV
The Buddy Type

9   Who is the Buddy Type?

WHAT ARE BUDDY TYPES LIKE?

People often mention how nice you are. It makes you feel good when you hear that and you like helping the people with whom you work. You always try to do your best and you're willing to put in extra time on a project and pitch in wherever it is needed even if it isn't strictly your job. After all, it's important you all work together to get the job done.

You like what you do. You work with some great people and you want to make sure you don't let them down. You like to keep people together by bringing in donuts on Fridays or starting a collection to buy a birthday cake. You know people appreciate little things like that. You like to feel comfortable in your office. Your group feels like old friends who look out for each other. Even when things are difficult, you can get through it if you all work together.

When people need help they come to you. Even people in other departments know if they need something, you'll do everything you can to help them. You see yourself as part of the big company team and believe when one department wins, you all win. You are not comfortable with the idea of company politics. Just the thought of it sounds underhanded and disturbs you. You firmly feel people should be rewarded for hard work and not for how well they play the office game. And you do work hard. Some days when you're the only person there at 7:00 PM, you think you work too hard, but then you remember it's your job. And you know it would be too difficult for them to get everything done without you.

You are very patient, especially with people who are trying something new. You really take the time to explain things thoroughly to others and encourage people to ask questions. You enjoy training people on new things and may often take the time to train new people yourself rather than have other people do it.

You pride yourself on your loyalty. Even when there are signals you should leave, you stay and hope things will get better. You want to be a loyal employee and you wonder sometimes why other people just bail out when things get tough.

You like to decorate your office or cubicle with personal items. Of course there are many photos of your family and friends, but there's also much more. Favorite pictures and stuffed animals and other things make the space your own. And you encourage your employees to decorate their cubicles in ways that make them feel at home. You believe that the more comfortable people are, the better they will perform. You may also have candy on your desk for people to nibble on when they stop by to chat.

You dress in a way that makes you feel comfortable also. You are not the power suit type. You prefer more relaxed, although professional, clothing, and if you have to wear a business suit, you typically add a special pin or scarf to soften the look. After all, you don't think it's necessary to look severe to get the job done.

When you make decisions, you make sure you weigh all the consequences very carefully. You find changes to be disruptive and stressful for everyone so great care is taken before you come to any decision that results in a change. Because of this, you often talk to other people about their opinions on a decision and, when possible, you prefer to make a group decision. You've heard group decisions are much better than individual decisions and you believe it to be true. Other people come up with good ideas you may not have thought of. And you also want to make sure you know how other people feel about the different available options especially if any change would affect them directly. You want to make sure everyone has had an opportunity to talk and feels heard before you make your final decision.

WHAT DOES THIS MEAN FOR YOU IN THE WORK-PLACE?

The good news is people think you do a good job and work very hard. The company depends on people like you to get the work done and to keep things flowing smoothly. When given a project, you take care of it. Your boss knows she can count on you to make sure there are no surprises. You will always stay within budget and do the best job you can even if it means sacrificing time and money from your own pet project to get things accomplished.

If you are a boss, the great news is most of your employees love working for you. Many have said that if you weren't there, they would leave the company. They see you as fair, approachable, supportive and generally a wonderful person for whom to work. They brag to their colleagues about what a great boss you are. The turnover in your department is the lowest in the company and human resources never gets complaints about the way you treat employees.

In addition, you feel like you have a great group. They really pitch in and help when needed. Even when someone is out sick, the rest of the people make sure the area is covered. Your department is such a nice place to work that several people have come to tell you they would like to work for you.

More good news is that you like what you do. You are good at it and to you, it's more than just a job. To you, it's your home away from home. You consider the people you work with to be your friends, and in some cases they feel like your extended family. You are comfortable with the people you work with. It's a good feeling and you wouldn't want it any other way.

❑ ❑ ❑ ❑ ❑ ❑ ❑ ❑

CASE STUDY # 3 — DESCRIPTION

Michelle (Buddy type)

Michelle is an Office Supervisor. She has worked at the same company for 9 years. She started as an office temporary and her job grew and grew. If you ask Michelle what her job is, she says she makes sure everything flows smoothly. She makes sure nothing goes wrong. Her unofficial motto is, "A happy employee is a great employee."

Michelle enjoys her job and is proud of the people with whom she works. She likes to hear about their children and has met most of their spouses at various company functions, like the company Holiday Party. She wants to know what is going on in people's lives and is surprised when some other employees don't want to talk about their family and hobbies. After all, she knows that Keith rides motorcycles on the weekends, Anne raises pedigree golden retrievers and Tricia has a waitress job on Friday nights so she can make enough money to go back to school. She also knows that Fred's wife is expecting twins, Carol is worried about her teenage son's friends and Saul is dating again after a particularly nasty divorce.

All the people who work with Michelle are important to her. She treats each person as an individual and she exhibits understanding and respect. She knows what each person likes: whether it's tickets to a baseball game, a nice bottle of wine or an afternoon off.

Stability is important to her and she doesn't like it when people leave. Her staff tends to be very loyal and stay with her a long time. Of course she knows that people left for other jobs to get more money and she wishes there was some way she could have offered more money so she could have kept some of the best people who quit.

WHAT SHE SAYS

It's not what Michelle says that sets her apart; it's what she doesn't say. She is an excellent listener. When she says her door is always open, she means it. No matter how busy she is, she is always willing to listen to one of her employees. Even if it means she won't be able to go home for hours, she'll be happy to listen to her employees share their concerns, whether work related or personal.

She doesn't interrupt when people talk to her. Sometimes people take a while to get to the point, but that's fine with her. There's a reason they feel the need to go into such detail and interrupting them would be rude.

Even when she's upset, she doesn't raise her voice. She has been disappointed when her employees have let her down, but she's never screamed at them. When Craig misplaced important information for a customer and didn't tell her right away, she called him in, closed the door and asked him what had happened. He knew she was upset and promised he would be more careful next time. Then she called the customer to smooth it over. She's glad things like that don't happen too often.

When she talks to her employees, she usually doesn't make too many bold statements. She likes to suggest ideas or she asks good questions to get other people to come up with their own solutions. When she wants someone to do something, she goes about it in a subtle way. And if the other person suggests a different way to do a project, Michelle will often let him or her try it.

WHAT SHE DOES

Michelle is great at thanking her staff. Some days she arrives early and puts a piece of candy on everyone's chair with a thank you note after a particularly difficult project. Often, after a busy week, she'll bring in her famous chocolate chip and walnut cookies to share with the staff. She's put together a lot of potluck lunches and finds they're a great way for people to get to know each other. That's just one of the many ways she tries to build a friendly and harmonious atmosphere at work.

You can find Michelle on Monday mornings asking everyone how his or her weekend was. She wants to know about cousin May's birthday party and Cindy's ballet recital. And she'll spend the time to hear about it too.

Michelle is predictable and dependable. She is at her desk every day. Even when she had pneumonia two years ago, she didn't want to stay home. She only missed work when her doctor ordered her to stay in bed.

RESULTS

Her department runs smoothly and she gets high productivity out of her group even though they are understaffed. Most of the people in Michelle's group are delighted to be working with her. They talk about how nice it is to be on a friendly team with no backstabbing.

Michelle is pleased to have such a supportive and helpful staff. She loves her job and can't imagine doing anything else.

10   Buddy Problems

Unfortunately, even though Buddy types are friendly people, problems can still exist at work. And when there are problems, they really bother you. Let's take a look at some common problems that you may see.

NOT BEING HEARD

As a Buddy type, you're uncomfortable with pushing your ideas or opinions on other people. You'd rather discuss something so you all can come to the same conclusion. Your way of persuading people is subtle and shows concern for the other person's feelings. But not everyone likes to communicate that way. You find that other people cut you off when you're trying to explain things. They're so busy trying to push their ideas that they don't have time to listen to yours. It's frustrating that so few people really take the time to talk and understand.

In meetings, your ideas are overlooked, too. You don't see opportunities for you to mention your viewpoint. And when you do suggest ideas, no one seems to notice them. Then to your surprise, a few minutes later someone mentions a similar idea that people like and everybody agrees with. You're glad people liked it, but you wish you had gotten the credit for coming up with it.

When you do take the time to really explain something in a meeting, you often get cut-off before you can finish. Some of your ruder colleagues just can't wait. They don't seem to see the importance of what you have to say. Is it any wonder that there are some meetings that you'd rather avoid? It seems like some of your colleagues just want to make fast decisions rather than really understand the underlying reasons and make the best decisions. Why can't they take a little more time? Why do they always have to be in such a rush? Why don't they ask people how they feel about the decisions?

In most of the meetings that you attend, you just end up sitting there and wondering if you should say something. Instead, it always seems that you come up with some great ideas after the meeting when you talk to people.

LACK OF LOYALTY

Sometimes Buddy types are unpleasantly surprised when the company isn't loyal to them. It's not unusual for someone else who you think is less loyal to be promoted ahead of you. And, unfortunately in these days of cost-cutting, it's not unexpected to have a Buddy type laid off after 15 or 20 years of loyal and earnest service. "It's nothing personal," says the company. Maybe it's not personal for them, but it's certainly personal for the Buddy types who tend to think of their workplaces like an extended family.

EXTRA WORK

Even though you love what you do, there are times that you wonder if people really appreciate the extra work you put in. Does it sometimes seem like you are the only one who really cares about some parts of a project and you are the only one willing to put in extra time to make it come out right? Do other people ask you to take on extra tasks that have little to do with your job because they know you'll say yes even if it means longer hours at the office for you?

You try to help others as much as you can, but sometimes it's hard to help them and to finish all of your work too. Still, you hate to say no. That just wouldn't fit in with the spirit of cooperation and you really wouldn't be comfortable with that. Of course you can't say yes to everything, and so there have been times that you've had to say no. And when that's happened, you've felt bad and carefully explained why you couldn't possibly help them even though you really wanted to.

Consider how your job affects you. Are there days that you feel tired and overwhelmed? Do you find yourself volunteering to take on additional tasks to help the group? What happens afterwards? You often end up taking on too many projects because you want to help other people and to be seen as a good team player. But then, you end up working late, pushing your other priorities to the side and start to feel resentful.

LACK OF RECOGNITION

Even though you work hard, you never seem to get the recognition from management that you deserve. You wait and hope for someone to notice your work and all the extra details and effort you put into it, but instead your colleagues get the credit and you are overlooked again and again. You don't seem to get your fair share of raises and promotions.

Sometimes it seems like the only people who get rewarded are loud hotshots who rudely brag about their own successes or sneaky people who know how to play company politics. You don't like to play those games; however, sometimes you wind up feeling like you're being taken for granted when you don't speak up. And worse, there are times when others take credit for your ideas. You know that you're doing a good job, but it would be nice to feel appreciated and acknowledged.

You wish there was something you could do about it, and there is. You can enjoy your job, have even better relationships with your employees and get rewarded for your hard work by making some simple, yet effective changes in the way you communicate with others.

◻ ◻ ◻ ◻ ◻ ◻ ◻ ◻

CASE STUDY # 3 — ISSUES

Michelle (Buddy type)

Michelle, the Office Supervisor, doesn't like conflict. The mere thought of conflict upsets her. Conflict makes problems for her whole department. That's why she works so hard to make sure that everyone likes to work together. When there is conflict, she tries to smooth it over rather than deal with it directly. She feels that dealing with it directly causes too many problems and can hurt her staff's feelings. She'd rather wait for things to calm down a bit before dealing with them.

A few people have complained about Michelle's inability to get resources for projects, hire additional people or give higher raises. It seems like other groups have supervisors who are willing to fight management for the things they need.

Michelle does talk to her boss, Robin, about what her department needs. Robin says that things are tight and she won't allocate money to hire additional people or to give higher raises to the people who are working extra hard. Michelle finds it hard to talk to Robin because she is so focused on the bottom line of the company. Michelle understands the company has a lot of competition in the market, but feels it's important to compensate those who work hard so they'll want to stay. Instead of talking with her boss further, she goes home and complains to her husband. She even tried to have the company pay for group lunches, but her boss said no, so Michelle has taken the group out to lunch using her own money.

Michelle is not too happy about her own salary. She has mentioned several times to Robin that she could use some extra money to go on a vacation and to put away for college for the

kids, but Robin quickly brushes the comments aside and changes the subject. Michelle gets a yearly increase, but it's not much. She'd like to get higher raises and sometimes she wonders if other people in the company are making more than she is. She knows that Robin says that times are tough, but it seems like the company is doing well and other managers continue to get promoted.

Robin knows that there is money in the budget, but she gives it to the supervisors and departments that fight for it. Robin gives Michelle raises every year, but she knows that she doesn't have to give her too much. Michelle might grumble a little bit but she's not going anywhere. She's loyal and dependable. Robin uses the extra money in the budget to keep people who she thinks might quit.

Conflicts in Michelle's group are often smoothed over until they get so big that people in other departments start to notice. For example, there was the time that Vickie kept coming in late. Michelle didn't mention it to her at first, hoping that Vickie would take care of it herself. But when Vickie started coming in 10–20 minutes late on most days, Michelle knew she had to do something. At first, Michelle tried to show Vickie that she noticed her tardiness by looking at the clock when Vickie passed by her desk in the morning. Unfortunately, Vickie didn't take the hint. Michelle then had to sit down with her and discuss it. Vickie explained that she was having a problem with her son at daycare and he cried every time she left so she had to stay later and later each day. Michelle sympathized and asked her to try harder. Unfortunately, the problem got worse until Robin finally mentioned it. After a few more discussions and a written warning, Vickie began to come to work on time. Vickie finally quit a few months later and Michelle still feels bad about the incident when she thinks about it and hopes Vickie didn't feel pushed out of her job.

At first, Vickie didn't think that her lateness was a problem. She figured that if it was a problem, Michelle would say something directly to her instead of hinting. After Michelle did finally mention the problem, Vickie didn't take it too seriously. She knew that Michelle would understand. When Vickie finally quit a few months later, she didn't feel pushed out. She thought that Michelle had been very nice about the whole situation.

Michelle is also having a problem with one of her other employees, Lorraine, who seems to be unfriendly. Lorraine does a good job but she doesn't like to join in with discussions that occur around the office. Michelle is worried that Lorraine doesn't like working there and has decided that she needs to get to know her better.

Lorraine likes to work by herself and doesn't see the need for her to spend time talking to other people when there's work to be done. Michelle has been talking to her more lately and asking about her personal life. That makes Lorraine uncomfortable and she wishes that Michelle would leave her alone and let her do her job.

Kelly, one of the sales people, is also a problem for Michelle. Kelly seems to stop by every week with a crisis that needs Michelle's attention. Michelle doesn't mind helping out now and then but it seems that Kelly causes some of her problems herself. Kelly rashly promises things to customers and if it's not in stock, then she needs Michelle's help to find it at one of the other locations. Michelle manages to figure out the problems and Kelly is very appreciative; however, she sometimes wishes that Kelly would take care of some of her own problems. If Kelly would just slow down a little, she could figure it out herself.

Kelly really appreciates Michelle handling all the details when she has a problem finding some parts. She hasn't had time to play around with the new computer system and isn't familiar with the process. Kelly knows that she should figure it out; however, Michelle's been so helpful that she hasn't needed to do it for herself. She knows that she can count on Michelle.

11   Toughening Up The Buddy Type

How do you feel about the information that you read in the past two chapters? Were you pleasantly surprised to read in Chapter 9 about how people really like to work with Buddy types? Did you feel a little uneasy when you read about potential problems in Chapter 10? If so, you are not alone. Most Buddy types know that they generally work well with others, but they also realize that there are some people with whom they can have problems.

So what can you do to get along well with everyone on the team while still being yourself? You don't want to learn to be tough, but you do want to be seen as someone who, with other people, can get things done. The way to do that is to understand what kinds of communication make other people comfortable. By understanding other people better, you can communicate in ways that are right for them and will make them more receptive to what you have to say.

Unfortunately, like most people, you tend to treat others the way that you would like to be treated, and that doesn't always work. You do have an advantage over some of the other types because, as a Buddy type, you are probably already in tune with what other people are feeling. You just need to use that information to focus on what makes them comfortable.

For example, if you have a co-worker who is a Brainy type and you sense she is having a bad day, you might try to get her to open up about what is bothering her. If someone did that for you, it would make you feel much better. Unfortunately, you need to understand that talking about her problems may not make your colleague feel better. Brainy types would rather minimize bad feelings by not talking about them. If you try to talk about her feelings, you might actually make her feel worse and she may try to avoid you. You will make it easier for her to communicate with you by not talking about her feelings.

You may be concerned that you'll have to make radical changes to communicate better with other people. Don't worry; there are many small changes you can make that will help people be more comfortable around you and allow them to hear what you have to say. Let's take a look at the different people you work with to see what you can do to communicate better with all of them.

WORKING WITH A BOSSY TYPE

You may have the biggest problems dealing with a Bossy type because you two are so different. Buddy types tend to show their emotions and are careful in making decisions. It's important for you to take people's feelings into account and weigh the outcomes. A Bossy type is very fast paced and wants to get right down to business. She doesn't want to hear about people's feelings. She wants to hear the bottom line, the net result, a brief summary.

When you talk to a Bossy type, she wants you to get right to the point. Her approach can often feel rude and abrupt, but you have to keep in mind that this type of communication is most comfortable for her.

Bossy types are typically very time-conscious, so you need to plan what you're going to say in advance. A good way to deal with a Bossy type is to write down the points you want to discuss before you talk to her. Then take a hard look at your list and delete any information that could be seen as extra details. When you have revised your list to where you feel it is as pared down as you dare go, pull out your red pen and delete even more. If you would normally take thirty minutes to give an update, you should try to cut it to five minutes. The problem is that you may not be sure what to take out because you think it's all of it is important.

Understanding how a Bossy type thinks can make it easier for you to prepare a proposal for her. When a Bossy type makes a decision, she trusts that it is a good decision. She expects the same from you. A Bossy type assumes that you have spent the time necessary to make a good decision before you present your plan to her, so she doesn't feel that she needs to hear all of the reasons that you considered. She trusts that you have gone through the appropriate process. She only wants to hear the results or the recommendations, nothing else.

Buddy types, on the other hand, want to make sure that everyone knows the reasons behind the decisions. If you don't give a full explanation, you may be afraid that someone else is not going to agree with you because they don't understand all of the data that you considered that led to your decision.

Bossy types, however, don't need as much information as you would like to give them. They prefer to get the bottom-line results or recommendations in quick bullet points. Bossy types want you to use short sentences and get right to the point. So when you are dealing with a Bossy type, you need to give her a very brief overview of the problem in a few short sentences and let her know what you feel are the best choices. Then STOP. Don't discuss what other people feel about your proposal unless it's absolutely necessary (such as the opinion of her boss or main customer). And don't explain background or historical information. If she wants it, trust that she'll ask for it.

Why should you do this? If you present the information in a way that a Bossy type can understand, then she will listen to you and take what you have to say into consideration. Typically when you walk into a Bossy type's office she's worried that you're going to take up a lot of her time with a long explanation and she may

look for ways to make you get to the point. She probably interrupts you often to get you to stop giving her what she feels is too
much information. She may say things like, "We've got to keep
this quick" or "I don't have time for a lot of talk, let's get on with
it" or "Just give me your conclusion". She is extremely time-conscious and she doesn't like it when she thinks you're wasting her
time even though you think the details are very important.

When you give her information that is quick and to the point,
she will appreciate it and will listen to it. If she feels it's too long,
she may lose interest and not focus on your suggestions. In addition, when you give the Bossy type information quickly, she will
be less likely to interrupt you and to try to rush you. That will
make you less frustrated when you deal with her.

It will most likely not feel comfortable to leave out the details
when speaking to a Bossy type. You may be concerned that the
Bossy type is not getting all of the information that she needs to
make the decision. That's fine with her. She doesn't want all the
information. She doesn't need all the background material
because she expects you to make the preliminary decision and
she'll do the rest.

For example, if you want to offer flexible scheduling for your
employees, you need to approach her in a bottom line way. You
may think that offering the option for employees to change their
hours would be a great benefit. Employees would appreciate the
opportunity to design a schedule where they could come in at
7:00 a.m. and leave at 3:00 p.m. You know that some of the
employees could really use this time to be with their kids or take
care of other personal business. However, to communicate
effectively with a Bossy type, it would be better if you didn't share
that information in your proposal.

Instead, you would quickly present the few key bottom line
business-related reasons that support why you should offer this

benefit. You could say that many other companies are successfully offering flexible schedules and you think your company should offer them also. It doesn't cost anything and other companies have experienced an increase in productivity and a reduction in absenteeism after introducing flexible scheduling. Don't spend time talking about what a great idea it is and how it will help the employees; just present the bottom line.

It might actually be better if you sent the Bossy type a short e-mail or memo listing key bullet points of the proposal instead of speaking with her directly so she wouldn't have to spend time talking about it. At the end of the message, you could offer to discuss the matter further if she needs additional information, but don't be surprised if she doesn't want to.

Overall you'll need to speed up and be more direct in your communication with a Bossy type. It may take some practicing with someone else or in front of a mirror but it's worth the time you take to get more comfortable talking to Bossy types so you can get better results.

WORKING WITH A BUBBLY TYPE

Bubbly types and Buddy types both tend to focus on Feelings. That can make it easier for you when you work with a colleague who's a Bubbly type. However, the ways that Bubbly types and Buddy types show emotions are very different. Bubbly types show their emotions in a more direct way. They might scream when they're mad and laugh loudly when they're delighted. Bubbly types are very comfortable talking about their feelings in large groups. You tend to be subtler with your feelings and prefer to relate to people one-on-one.

Bubbly types are friendly and talkative; however, their pace is much faster than yours. They will often interrupt you and finish your sentences for you. Bubbly types are Action-oriented. They are quick and want to rush ahead. As a Buddy type, you want to take time to really get to know people in a more meaningful way.

Bubbly types like to generate enthusiasm and motivate other people. They like to be entertaining. They like creative ideas. If you are working on a project together, let them handle the creative part or suggest they lead a brainstorming session. When you deal with a Bubbly type, you need to realize that she likes to be the center of attention; so let her have the spotlight.

When you work with a Bubbly type, you should appeal to her need for excitement, creativity and sense of fun. For example, if you want to get a Bubbly type to agree to start offering flexible schedules to the employees, you'll want to talk about how much the employees will love the idea and how it will increase their motivation. Having happy employees is very important to a Bubbly type. You may also suggest to the Bubbly type that she make the announcement about the new program at a major company event that will highlight the company's commitment to people. That would make her the center of attention and allow her to share her excitement with others at the same time.

The most important things that you need to do with a Bubbly type are speed up, share her enthusiasm and have fun with her.

WORKING WITH ANOTHER BUDDY TYPE

You may think that working with another Buddy type would be easy and in many cases, you're right. It is easy. Another Buddy type has the same concerns that you do. Two Buddy types working together, though, may be so comfortable that they don't get the work done. You may have lots of meetings where you talk and feel connected but don't really handle the issues. Or you may both be so nice that you don't want to bring up any unpleasant problems because that might mean conflict.

When you work with another Buddy type, you should enjoy it.

It's refreshing to talk to someone else who really understands you. At the same time, you need to make sure that you focus on the problem you're working on and take action.

WORKING WITH A BRAINY TYPE

You have something in common with the Brainy types with whom you work. You both like to work at a slower pace than the Bossy types and Bubbly types; however, your focus is different. You think it's important to take the time to understand the people around you and to build solid relationships. A Brainy type thinks it's important to understand the facts.

Brainy types are more solitary than you are and are reluctant to discuss personal information. You need to respect that and make sure you don't ask about their personal lives or tell them too much about yourself. Brainy types tend to be more comfortable with written communication than discussions, so you may want to write letters or e-mail rather than pick up the phone to talk to them. Whatever method you use to give information to Brainy types, it needs to be presented in a logical and organized format. Because such structure is not your natural inclination, it is important that you take the time to put your thoughts together in an orderly manner before speaking to a Brainy type. Brainy types tend to be highly organized and they expect the same from you.

When you work on a project with Brainy types, you need to keep in mind that their top priority is to understand the facts. They are concerned about details and order. They want to know the background and history of a project, and they want to make sure that the rules and regulations are followed. You both want to focus on details but your details include information on people; whereas, the details that are more important for Brainy types are numerical or procedure based. Brainy types need to take time to carefully plan to make sure they don't make mistakes and they need time alone to concentrate.

When you give information to a Brainy type, it is best to take the feelings out of it. Brainy types rely on charts and graphs and numbers, not on personal stories. If you want to show how people feel about something, it will be more acceptable if you can focus on the numbers rather than the stories. For example, if you are trying to convince a Brainy type to offer flexible schedules for employees, it would not be effective if you gave details about how much some of the people in the office really want flexible scheduling and how much it would boost morale. Instead, translate the information into numerical details and say that 24 out of the 25 people in the office said "yes" when asked in a survey if they thought that flexible scheduling was a good option for companies to offer and the 25th person said "maybe". Then show how other companies have done it and what their numerical results have been.

The next step would be to do an analysis of the costs involved. In this example, there are no costs involved and that should be highlighted when speaking to the Brainy type. Then you should provide the details of the procedures, how this would be put into place, and what results you anticipate for the company. This organized and logical information will be much more convincing than a detailed story of how wonderful flexible schedules would be and how they would help improve your employees' qualities of lives. It would be even better if you wrote this information down in a report with clear and logical reasons supporting your conclusion and charts showing results from other companies.

What you should remember most about dealing effectively with Brainy types is that they need processes and numbers given to them in a logical and orderly manner. They want to focus on the Facts, not the Feelings, and they expect you to do the same.

CHECKLIST FOR GETTING ALONG BETTER WITH DIFFERENT TYPES

With The Bossy Type:

✓Give yourself permission to trust yourself and your decisions. Remember that you know what's best for your group. That will help you from getting flustered when the Bossy type asks you questions.

✓Keep your meeting very brief and focus only on the recommendations. You can ask if the Bossy type would like to know the details of how you decided on the recommendations but don't expect her to say yes.

✓Don't worry if the Bossy type doesn't want to know the details. If that happens, it doesn't mean she doesn't care. It shows that she trusts your decision-making abilities.

With The Bubbly Type:

✓When preparing to speak with a Bubbly type, remember what is important to her: fun, creativity, spontaneity, excitement and motivation. With this in mind, check your proposal to see if it includes some fun and exciting information.

✓Be prepared to spend time brainstorming and chatting about the idea.

✓Your enthusiasm about the idea is very important in getting a Bubbly type to follow your lead. If you're not enthusiastic about the idea, then it may be hard for the Bubbly type to work on it.

With The Buddy Type:

✓Add some extra time to your meetings so you can chat and won't feel rushed.

✓Before meeting with another Buddy type, prepare a

checklist of the few main items to cover so you can keep referring to them and to keep you both on track. It's so easy when talking to each other to lose focus on the reason for the meeting. Keep reminding each other to get back to business.

✓Make sure you leave enough time at the end of the meeting to decide on specific actions that each one of you will take as a result of your discussion.

With The Brainy Type:

✓Be prepared to explain all the reasons behind your proposal, but remember to organize your information in a logical and structured manner, making sure that you leave out any emotional information about your idea.

✓Focus on the facts and include as many numbers and statistics as possible to support your ideas.

✓Be sure to give the Brainy type plenty of time to think about your plan and study the information alone. Don't worry if she doesn't get back to you right away. A Brainy type needs time to digest new ideas before coming to any conclusions.

◻ ◻ ◻ ◻ ◻ ◻ ◻ ◻

CASE STUDY # 3 — SOLUTIONS

Michelle (Buddy type)

Michelle was happy to learn about the 4 Bs. She was fascinated to find a system that would help her to really understand the other people in her work group. She felt that her boss, Robin, was a Bossy type because of her fast actions and her focus on the business instead of the people. Michelle realized that in order to get what she needed from Robin she was going to have to be direct and persistent. Michelle was uncomfortable with that; however, she decided that she really needed to get a budget for salary increases for her best performers.

Before talking to Robin, Michelle put together a bottom-line presentation about what would happen if her employees left. She cut the information to the barest minimum and sent Robin a brief e-mail with just a few bullet points asking directly for 5% increases for all her employees. She had to remind Robin about it two more times before Robin said that she would consider it.

Robin reviewed Michelle's information and thought she had some good points. Before Robin agreed to the increases, she wanted to wait to make sure that Michelle was really serious. Michelle's persistence showed Robin that she was willing to fight for it.

Michelle reviewed Lorraine's work and decided that she was a Brainy type. Michelle realized that Lorraine was happy working by herself and did not need to be included in all the discussions. Michelle also realized that as a Brainy type, Lorraine was not comfortable talking about any personal information, hers or anyone else's. Michelle decided to leave her alone and let her do her work.

Lorraine was relieved when Michelle stopped trying to chat with her. After all, work is work and there's no place for personal life there.

Michelle tried to be a little more direct with Kelly (a Bubbly type). She let Kelly know that she would be happy to help her get set up to learn the computer process so she could handle her own problems. She helped Kelly get excited about the process by telling her about all of the other things she could also do on the computer. When Kelly said she didn't have time, she and Michelle brainstormed ways to get the time for training.

Kelly was enthusiastic about learning the new system but she still wished that Michelle would handle all of the details for her. She really liked working with Michelle.

Michelle felt good about how she was able to communicate with people who were different from her. She felt her new skills could help her to understand the people around her and would make an even better work environment.

V
The Brainy Type

12 Who is the Brainy Type?

Brainy types focus on Facts and prefer Thinking over Action. Brainy types are:

1. Calm
2. Quiet
3. Private
4. Detail Oriented
5. Logical & Structured

Let's review each of these descriptions.

1. CALM

As a Brainy type, you're proud of the fact that you control your emotions. Even though you may have strong feelings about a topic, you are determined to display limited emotions at work. You think it's important to always stay calm and cool, especially in difficult situations. Even when you are angry, it takes a lot for you to lose your temper. When you're mad, you prefer to withdraw rather than yell at someone.

When you deal with people problems, you focus on the facts rather than the feelings. You are proud of your ability to see situations objectively even when other people become emotional. You do your best to make decisions without being swayed by unnecessary information.

2. QUIET

You are much quieter than the Bubbly types and Bossy types with whom you work. You don't boast about your accomplishments because you would rather let your hard work speak for itself.

You think carefully before you give your opinions. You need

time to make sure that you are correct. You are reluctant to make suggestions unless you have all of the facts. To others, this may make you appear lacking in confidence; however, you would rather wait to talk then try to make a guess.

Some people whom you work with like to talk and talk. You don't feel the need to chat and you conserve your words for when you really have something important to say.

You work well on your own and you thrive in an atmosphere that is quiet and free of distractions. An office with a closed door is a great way to support the concentration that is necessary for doing a thorough job.

3. PRIVATE

You are a very private person and have a hard time understanding why other people with whom you work want to share all of the details of their personal lives. You don't mind telling people general information, such as where you went over the weekend, but you certainly would never share intimate stories about your family life. It is embarrassing to hear others talk about their private issues in the office and you try to avoid conversations that become too personal. You don't need to know that much about the people at work. You wish that other people would keep their personal lives to themselves.

Even though you are cordial with your co-workers, you think that your company is not a place to develop friendships. You tend to keep most of your conversations focused on work. When you arrive at the office on Monday morning, you go right to your desk and start on your To Do list instead of asking people what they did on Saturday night.

4. DETAIL ORIENTED

When the people in your company need something done that

involves a lot of details, they give it to a Brainy type. You handle information carefully and make sure that nothing gets missed. You often create long To Do lists and prioritize tasks to make sure that every point is covered.

To you, perfection is not just a virtue; it is a way of life. You are extremely thorough and carefully review everything to make sure that it is correct before giving it to anyone else. Your finished products are neat and precise.

5. LOGICAL & STRUCTURED

You approach your work in a logical manner. While other people around you may use "gut feelings" to make decisions, you rely solely on good data and careful analysis. You make decisions by gathering information and analyzing it until you reach a conclusion that makes sense.

Your analysis includes as much historical information as possible, since past performance can be a good indicator of what will happen in the future. You want to know what happened last year and the year before that. If you can gather the information from the past 10 or 20 years, then you can be more confident in your decisions.

You need as much information as possible, and you are willing to delay decisions until you are 100% sure of your answers. You don't want to make mistakes.

You work best with structure and prefer to take things step by step. You don't approve of "cutting corners" and you take the time necessary to make sure that work is done properly. You like to put things in order and if there is no structure, then you create some. You often develop carefully constructed flow charts and work plans to make sure that all deadlines are met.

Following schedules makes work much easier for you. You are punctual and expect the same of others. When you tell someone else to meet you at 1:00, you don't mean 1:05.

You are predictable and stable. Your colleagues always know what to expect from you.

Overall, you are analytical and structured. People count on you for your thoroughness and attention to detail.

◻ ◻ ◻ ◻ ◻ ◻ ◻ ◻

CASE STUDY # 4 — DESCRIPTION

Tanya (Brainy type)

Tanya is a Sales Associate for a company that sells office supplies. She has worked at the company for four years. She supports five regional sales managers and helps them to take care of customer orders. She is responsible for shipping the orders, sending out invoices and dealing with customer problems when the sales managers aren't available.

Tanya is very proud of the tracking system that she put in place, which makes it easy for her to see the status of every order at each stage of the shipping process. She is detail-oriented, serious, careful and neat. She doesn't like sloppy work.

When she gets calls from angry customers, Tanya calms them down and focuses on the facts. She analyzes the problems and gets back to the customers with complete information.

Tanya gets along with the other members of her group, but she doesn't spend time chit-chatting when she has work to do. Sometimes she eats lunch with the people she works with and some days she needs to unwind by reading a magazine at her desk while she eats.

Tanya's boss, Beth, praises her for her thoroughness and has said that when Tanya works on a project, everything is done perfectly. Tanya is pleased that her hard work has been noticed and is starting to think about the next step for her career.

13   Brainy Problems

Unfortunately some of the Brainy characteristics that we looked at in the last chapter can lead to problems at work. Let's examine them one at a time.

1. CALM

You have strong feelings; however, you do not choose to show them at work. You are good at controlling your emotions and you expect everyone else to be able to do the same.

Bubbly types and Buddy types expect you to openly show how you feel. They may complain that you are detached and unapproachable. They see you as too stiff and formal. They may suggest that you "loosen up" and relax. They like to develop relationships with the people they work with and your stoic behavior can be seen as unfriendly.

2. QUIET

Quiet people in companies tend to be overlooked. Attention seems to go to people who loudly proclaim their accomplishments. You can't expect your work to speak for itself. You need to find ways to let people know about your hard work so that you get rewarded.

You have problems being heard in meetings. You are reluctant to interrupt with your thoughts and so your ideas may not be included. And if you are directly asked to comment about something brought up in a meeting, you don't like to make statements until you've had a chance to think about it. That can make you look like you are not confident or that you don't know what you are doing.

In meetings, quick responses tend to be rewarded whether they are correct or not.

It also causes you great frustration in meetings when the group decides to "brainstorm" ideas. To you, that is a complete waste of time. You can't imagine that you'll be able to come up with a solution by just tossing out ideas without giving them appropriate thought and study. In brainstorming sessions, you tend to hold back so your ideas don't get included. You may try to offer your input after the meeting when you've had time to analyze the data, but it may be too late because the group has already made a decision.

You like to work by yourself because you can get so much done when you are not interrupted. It gives you time to think and analyze issues. Unfortunately, working alone can make it appear that you are not team-oriented. In most organizations, you need to work with other people to get things done.

3. PRIVATE

You don't like it when other people bring their personal problems to work. You don't bother other people with your problems and you don't want to know about your co-workers' personal lives. When they tell you intimate information, they get offended when you don't seem interested.

Often you may find yourself eating lunch in front of your computer while your more friendly colleagues go to lunch together. That may not bother you because it allows you to get more work done. But in order to get things accomplished in the business world, you need to develop good relationships with your co-workers.

4. DETAIL-ORIENTED

In some jobs, attention to detail is absolutely required. As you move up in organizations, jobs tend to require more focus on strategy. If you become known as someone who is great at details but can't see the big picture, you will limit how far you can go in the company or in your career.

Your desire to be 100% correct and to turn in perfect work can cause you to move too slowly. You can develop an "analysis paralysis," where you can't make decisions until you get enough data. You may put off decisions for months while you try to find the last bit of information that will confirm your decisions. This means that you could miss out on opportunities. You will also annoy the Bossy types and Bubbly types with whom you work because they want to make decisions as quickly as possible.

You are great at analyzing data but you may not be good at doing something with it. You prefer to think and think about something rather than take action. That can be seen as a negative in action-oriented companies.

5. LOGICAL & STRUCTURED

Your focus on logic may cause problems with other people. When you make decisions, you need to include more than just the hard facts. You do need to include people's feelings and concerns. When it comes to analyzing numbers, you are great, but when it comes to analyzing other people, you find them confusing.

Your need for structure can make it hard for you to make changes. Once you make plans, you want to stick with them. To others, you may appear rigid and inflexible when they suggest changes that you did not anticipate.

When you get information, your focus is on the past, what was done before, and how you can you learn from it. When the economy is changing rapidly, focusing on the past can lead to poor decisions. In today's business world, you can't assume that what worked six months ago will work the same way now and in the future.

Fortunately for you, there are steps you can take to make communication easier with your co-workers. In the next chapter, we'll see how you can analyze the communication needs of other types so that you can respond appropriately.

◻ ◻ ◻ ◻ ◻ ◻ ◻ ◻

CASE STUDY # 4 — ISSUES

Tanya (Brainy type)

Even though Tanya does well at her job, she does have problems with Grace, one of the sales managers. Grace wants to try some new packaging that she thinks will make the products look better. Grace is excited about it and thinks that customers will really love it. Tanya is reluctant to try it because she can't see any logical reason to change. The current packaging works fine. She told Grace that she would research what the change would mean and give her a comparison as soon as she can find out all the information.

Grace can't believe that Tanya is so focused on unimportant details. This is what the customers want and that will mean more sales. Can't Tanya see that? Grace can't wait for a long analysis. She wants to try the new packaging now before their competitors do.

Tanya's boss, Beth, praises Tanya for her accuracy; however, she is concerned that Tanya spends too much time focusing on details. Beth is also concerned that Tanya is not a team player. Tanya is not sure how to handle that. When she asked Beth for more information, Beth suggested that Tanya should spend more time talking with the other people in the office. That didn't make any sense to Tanya because if she spent more time talking, it would make it hard for her to get all her work done.

Beth is afraid that Tanya's rigid ways are alienating the other members of the team. She wants Tanya to understand that she can't just focus on facts. She has to understand that she is dealing with people.

Tanya also has a problem with Lizzette, one of her customers. Lizette is impatient and rude. When Lizette has a problem with a missing order, she doesn't want to hear about Tanya's shipping process. Lizette says that she just wants Tanya to do whatever is necessary to get her orders to her the next day. Tanya dreads talking to her.

Lizette doesn't have time to hear about Tanya's tracking process. She just wants to know what Tanya is going to do to solve her problem.

Tanya is frustrated and she wonders if she would be better off at another company that values high-quality work.

14   Getting the Brainy Type to Feel

The first thing that you need to realize is that everyone communicates differently. You need to determine if the person you are communicating with is a Bossy type, Bubbly type, Buddy type or Brainy type. One way to do that is to follow the flow chart in the Appendix.

When you determine the appropriate communication style, the next step is to re-formulate your message in a way that is more consistent with how the other person tends to communicate. In this chapter, you will get examples of some steps you can take to structure your communication more effectively.

You will find some of the steps easier than others, depending on you and your situation. You do not need to follow all of the steps in order to see improvement. You may improve communication by trying just one step.

Let's analyze each communication type:

1. BOSSY TYPE
Bossy types focus on Facts and are Action-oriented. Here is how they compare to Brainy types:

Fact Focus
You and the Bossy type both focus on Facts. You know that the Bossy type is going to want to work on the task and not let people issues get in the way.

Action Orientation
Bossy types want to take Action, but you are more Thinking-oriented. Bossy types tend to be louder and more forceful than you

are. In order to communicate well, you must act in a more assertive way than you usually do.

Bossy types value fast decisions and quick results. They don't spend much time reviewing details. They communicate about the big picture and prefer to get their information delivered to them in just a few bullet points.

Process

The steps listed below will help you to communicate more clearly with a Bossy type.

1. Speak faster.

2. Get to the point right away. Plan your conversation with a Bossy type by analyzing the one or two main points. Give her that information instead of all the background and process explanations.

3. Focus on the big picture, not details. What do the details add up to? What is the overall information? Give this information to the Bossy type and keep the details to yourself.

4. Make decisions without 100% of the information. Analyze the minimum amount of information you actually need to be confident that the decision will be correct. You must realize that you cannot expect that you will always be right. It is acceptable to make changes if the decision does not work out the way you had planned.

Example

If you are trying to convince a Bossy type to purchase a new software system, you should speed up your presentation, quickly get to the main point and avoid giving too many details. Bossy types hate to waste time and want information presented to them with limited alternatives.

For example, if you have researched nine different software systems and reviewed each one on price, compatibility with the current system, after-sale support and expected training costs, do not give all that information to the Bossy type. Just briefly tell her the top one or two recommendations and the bottom-line cost. Don't talk about the details or the process you went through to get the information. If she wants details, she'll ask for them.

2. BUBBLY TYPE

Of all the people you work with, Bubbly types are the most difficult. They seem to do the opposite of what you do. You prefer Thinking and they prefer to take Action. You are focused on Facts and they are focused on Feelings. It will not be easy; however with careful planning you can deal with the differences. Here is how Bubbly types compare to Brainy types:

Feeling Focus

Bubbly types show emotions in very obvious ways. In order for Bubbly types to be more comfortable dealing with you, you must show more emotion. That could include smiling more often and showing enthusiasm for their ideas. You can also get along better with a Bubbly type by making jokes and acting less serious. Bubbly types like to have fun and they prefer to work with people who they think are friendly and exciting.

Ask about the Bubbly type's personal life. You don't need to get too personal. For example, on Monday morning, instead of heading immediately to your desk, you could ask your co-workers about their weekends. What did they do? Was it fun? Then you could join in and describe what you did over the weekend. Share some personal stories about how you spent time with your family. It may not seem appropriate, but Bubbly types want to get to know you as a person so they can work with you better.

Action Orientation

When you deal with Bubbly types, you must speed up your communication. Bubbly types like to talk and work fast. They are not comfortable with silence and if no one else is talking, they may continue to talk just to fill the silence. You may wonder if they are ever going to shut up so you can talk. They may wonder if you are ever going to say something. They usually will not pause long enough for you to add your comments so you need to learn to interrupt them. It doesn't seem right, however, it is often the best way to get the information across. Bubbly types typically don't mind being interrupted as long as it moves the conversation forward. They want other people to communicate with them even if their constant talking makes it seem like they don't want to listen to anyone else.

In order to communicate clearly, you need to make direct statements instead of suggesting information or asking questions. Bubbly types often do not react to subtle hints so you need to very clearly explain what you are saying.

Bubbly types generally don't like to work with a lot of details. They like to talk about the big picture. The best way to deal with this is to handle the details yourself without bothering the Bubbly type.

Bubbly types are not comfortable with structure. They complain that it's too confining and they prefer to "wing it". If you are working with a Bubbly type, you need to resist the urge to bring order and structure to her part of the project unless she asks for your help.

Process

The steps listed below will help you to communicate more clearly with a Bubbly type.

    1. Smile and make jokes.

    2. Speak faster.

3. Be enthusiastic about the projects on which she is working.

4. Discuss the big picture, not the details.

5. When asked for information, don't supply charts and graphs—give your best estimates. During brainstorming sessions, jump in with your suggestions.

6. Ask about her personal life. Show an interest in her life outside of the office. Ask about her family and friends.

7. Share personal information. You don't need to talk about intimate details. Just talk about your hobby or what you did over the weekend.

Example

If you want to convince a Bubbly type to agree to a new software system, you need to present it in a way that gets her excited and interested. For example, you may want to talk about how the system you suggest is the best or the newest or the most sophisticated. Discuss how the new system will motivate employees by making their jobs much easier.

Don't bring up the details, unless the Bubbly type asks you. And if she does ask for details, keep them to a minimum.

3. BUDDY TYPE

Buddy types focus on Feelings and are Thinking-Oriented. This is how Buddy types compare to Brainy types:

Feelings Focus

This is why you may have problems dealing with Buddy types. Buddy types focus on people and relationships where you focus on facts.

Buddy types want to get to know the people with whom they work. They like to find out who you are and how you feel. This makes it easier for them to understand you and be comfortable working with you. So you need to tell a Buddy type a little about yourself and you need to ask about her personal life.

Buddy types like to share personal feelings after they get to know you. They relate to people by sharing their concerns. Don't try to solve their problems, just listen.

While you prefer to work alone, Buddy types prefer to work in a team. They make sure that everyone on the team is included and that each person's feelings are considered.

Thinking-Oriented

You share this trait with Buddy types. They often communicate in a quiet way and take their time giving information. Buddy types often are reluctant to give out information unless they are sure that you really want it, especially if it's not good news. You will need to draw it out of them by asking questions.

Process

1. Smile more.

2. Work with a group of people. Buddy types don't like to work alone. (Be sure to schedule time for you to work on your own.)

3. Share some personal information about yourself.

4. Ask them for personal information.

5. Ask how they are feeling—about a certain project or about their mood in general. Buddy types may not immediately reveal their feelings, but they appreciate being asked. Once they become more comfortable with you, they will be happy to share their feelings.

6. Ask how other people are feeling. Buddy types like to work with other people and they like to make sure that others' concerns are addressed.

Example

If you want to convince a Buddy type to agree to a new software system, you need to consider how it will affect other people in the group. Involve as many people as possible in the decision and let the Buddy type know how other people feel about it. Buddy types want to make sure that everyone's concerns are addressed, so you need to explain how you will deal with anyone who is worried about the new software.

Be sure to check with the Buddy type to see how she feels about the project. Make sure you deal with her reactions and reassure her that you are listening to her concerns.

4. BRAINY TYPE

In general it is easy to work with another Brainy type; however, you need to be aware of a potential problem. Sometimes when two Brainy types get together, they focus too much on the details. They may spend so much time analyzing and reviewing that they take too long to finish and miss opportunities. Remember, when you work with another Brainy type, you need to set deadlines so that you stop analyzing and take action.

STRUCTURES FOR DEALING WITH DIFFERENT TYPES

For the Bossy type:
Be Action-Oriented.
> 1. Get to the point quickly.
> 2. Make direct statements.

For the Bubbly type:
Focus on Feelings.
> 1. Show emotions.
> 2. Be aware of other people's emotions.

Be Action-Oriented.
>   1. Give few details.
>   2. Speed up.

For the Buddy type:
Focus on Feelings.
>   1. Ask for other people's opinions.
>   2. Ask how the Buddy type is feeling.

For the Brainy type:
>   1. Develop a reasonable project schedule and limit time for analysis.
>   2. Don't get so bogged down in the details that you miss the big picture.

◻ ◻ ◻ ◻ ◻ ◻ ◻ ◻

CASE STUDY #4 — SOLUTIONS

Tanya (Brainy type)

After learning about the 4 Bs, Tanya thought about how she could use it with the people with whom she works.

Tanya agreed to try out the new packaging that Grace (a Bubbly type) wanted. Tanya didn't like making a change without appropriate data, but Grace was absolutely sure that the customers would love it. Tanya realized that even if this was not the right decision, they could go back to the old packaging without too much trouble.

Grace was very excited by Tanya's willingness to go ahead with the new packaging. Grace realized that Tanya was not as rigid as she had thought.

Tanya decided that Beth, her boss, was a Buddy type. She asked Beth to meet with her to discuss how to be a better team player.

After the meeting, Tanya spent more time talking with the other people in the group and made it a point to join them for lunch.

Beth was pleased by Tanya's willingness to work together with the team. Tanya has made a real effort to get along better with her co-workers.

The next time that Lizette (a Bossy type) called, Tanya quickly said that she would look into the problem call her back. When Tanya returned the call, she got right to the point and said that the shipment would arrive the next day. Tanya still didn't like dealing with Lizette, but it was much better than previous conversations.

Lizette got the answers she wanted without having to hear all of the details.

After analyzing her job situation, Tanya decided to stay and improve her communication skills. This new information helped her to get ready for the next step in her career.

VI
Becoming Successful

15   The 4 Bes for the 4Bs

Now that you know a little more about yourself and the people at work, what should you do? First, by knowing how other people perceive you, you can deal with negative views that people may have of you. Second, you can be a better communicator by learning to be more flexible. Third, you can pick one relationship that you would like to improve with better communication.

1) DEALING WITH NEGATIVE VIEWS

Review the negative information in the chapters that describe you. Which negative descriptions apply to you? For example, if you are a Bubbly type, you might admit that you are not too organized. (You might even have seen that as a strength, since you are so busy you don't have time to be organized. Now you can see how other people might see it as a weakness.) You may feel organized; however, if you take an unbiased look at your office, you can admit that the many piles of paper would look disorganized to a Brainy type.

When you understand your weaknesses, you can begin to make small adjustments in how you work with other people so they see you in a different way. If you are a Bubbly type and you think people may perceive that you are disorganized, you can straighten up your office or arrive on time to meetings. If you are a Brainy type, and you realize that people may think you are too serious, you can consider ways to lighten up a bit. You may want to make a few jokes or plan a celebration lunch with your co-workers.

By looking at your real and perceived weaknesses, you can begin to break through the stereotypes so that people can see you for the multi-talented person that you are.

2) BECOMING MORE FLEXIBLE — LEARNING NEW LANGUAGES

We mentioned in the beginning that learning about different communication types is like learning new languages. When you learn the language of Buddy types or Brainy types, it makes it easier for you to get your points across. It also makes it easier for them to hear what you have to say. It doesn't mean that you have to be fluent or that you must become a Buddy type, but it does mean that you have to learn some basic phrases. Think of this book as a phrase book that you can pull out when you need help in translating what someone else is saying.

This information will only help you to understand people in a general way. Each person is unique. It's up to you to get to know people as individuals once you learn their basic languages.

3) WORK ON YOUR MOST IMPORTANT RELATIONSHIP

You might be overwhelmed with all of the information and think that you can never use it all at one time. You don't need to. The best way for you to start using this information is to just focus on dealing with one person at a time. Instead of trying to learn all the different languages for the different types, just focus on one. Would you try to learn Spanish, German and Chinese all at the same time? No, it would get too confusing.

The best way to decide which communication type to work on first is to ask yourself, "Who is the most important person that I deal with?" Is it your boss? Is it a key customer? That's the person who you need to focus on when you first use this information. Pick that one key person and use your new knowledge to figure out that person's general style. Use that as a starting point to understand how to communicate with her better.

Once you decide who you need to have a better relationship with, you still might feel overwhelmed with all of the information. For example, if your boss is a Buddy type, you might be wondering how you can be subtle and friendly and speak slower and add more pauses in the conversations and be team oriented all at the same time. It seems like too much to worry about. So don't try to do everything at once. You should start out slow. Just pick one or two things to work on. Remember, you don't need to make major changes; you just need to make small adjustments.

USE THE 4BES OF COMMUNICATION

To be a better communicator, follow the 4 Bes: Be Aware, Be Yourself, Be Courageous and Be Persistent.

Be Aware

The first and most important step in becoming a better communicator at work is to be aware of your own communication type and the effect that it has on other people. How do people see you? Look at how people react to you. With whom do you communicate well and with whom do you have problems? Are you happy with the results or do you want to make some improvements? By making changes in the way you deal with people, you can get much better results, have more fun, develop better relationships and be more successful.

Be Yourself

It's important to understand that you should only make small adjustments that will help other people be more comfortable with you. Don't become a completely different person. You should be yourself, only more flexible.

When you decide that you do want to make some adjustments, you should start small and pick something easy at first. Don't overwhelm yourself by planning to make lots of changes all at once. It's better to focus on one or two areas that you think you can easily adjust.

Some of the suggestions in this book may not make sense to you or don't feel right to you. Then pick something else. You should only do what works for you personally.

Make the changes specific. If you are a Bubbly type, don't just decide that you are going to communicate better with a Brainy type. Instead, choose one specific thing that you can commit to doing. You may decide the one thing you can do is to slow down when you talk to the Brainy type. Just by making that one small adjustment, you can increase communication dramatically.

Be Courageous

Try it. It's easy to read about changing the way you communicate, but it's hard to actually try something that's less than comfortable for you. You might be afraid that you'll fail. Don't let that stop you from trying new approaches. You'll find the results will be worth it.

When you try something for the first time, it may feel strange. Just because something seems a little awkward doesn't mean that you should abandon it right away. Keep trying until you get better at it and it feels more natural. It takes strength and courage to try something new. Take a deep breath and don't be afraid to try something new.

Be Persistent

I have bad news for you. There are going to be times when this information doesn't work. When you have problems using this information, you should review the situation. Maybe the change you've picked is too difficult for you or maybe you have misjudged what will work with a particular person. Should you stop trying because of one problem? Of course not. When you were a child and you first tried to walk, you didn't give up when you fell down. If you did, you'd still be crawling. Keep trying until you get the results you want.

SUMMARY:

For Bossy Types:

✓Be Aware—See the effect you have on other people.

✓Be Yourself—Only make small changes.

✓Be Courageous—Push yourself to do things that aren't comfortable.

✓Be Persistent—Don't give up even when you think this is taking too long to get results.

For Bubbly Types:

✓Be Aware—Look around you at the people you work with and see the effect that you have on them. Most people think you're terrific and really enjoy working with you! ☺ Imagine what you can do to have a better relationship with everyone.

✓Be Yourself—You are a happy, fun person. ☺ Just remember that for some people, you may come across as too enthusiastic or overly optimistic and they may not appreciate it. You may have to tone down your energy a little bit in order to get along with others.

✓Be Courageous—You like to try new things, so experiment. Have fun with it! It will give you a chance to be creative in how you relate to other people.

✓Be Persistent—Instead of trying many things like you usually do, try to pour your energies into one area. When you succeed in that area, then you can move on to something else!

For Buddy Types:

✓Be Aware—You are very aware of yourself and others around you. You really understand how other people feel.

Use this awareness to look at the relationships you have with your co-workers. What do you do that makes people comfortable and what do you do that may sometimes make them uncomfortable? Use your understanding of how other people feel to get along with them better.

✓Be Yourself—You don't need to change the caring person that you are in order to be a better communicator with difficult people. It's helpful for you to realize that not everyone is comfortable communicating the way you do and it's okay for you to approach communication in different ways. You can learn to use your strengths to further develop relationships with others.

✓Be Courageous—You are cautious about change so it's not easy for you to try new things until you feel comfortable. You may want to try talking with people whom you trust so they can help you to consider what would work for you. They can also give you support and encouragement that will make it easier for you to explore new ways of doing things.

✓Be Persistent—You are good at sticking with things once you make up your mind. If you find that you are struggling, you can ask for some suggestions from others. By enlisting other people to help you, it makes it easier to keep going.

For Brainy Types:

✓Be Aware—Look objectively at how other people may view your actions. List the areas that you would like to change.

✓Be Yourself—Prioritize the changes that you could make according to what is easiest for you to do and what is hardest.

✓Be Courageous—Use your planning skills to determine

the next logical steps. After careful consideration, take specific actions.

✓Be Persistent—If something doesn't work, review the information and determine what went wrong and what needs to be changed for the next time.

Now that you understand how you naturally communicate, it would be helpful to find out how your co-workers communicate. The most accurate way is to ask them to take the quiz and let you know their scores. If you can't do that, you can get a good idea of their preferred communication type by scoring them on the Understanding Others Quiz listed below.

Remember, since this is based on your impressions, it won't be completely accurate. When you finish the quiz, you can test your perceptions by trying out the suggestions from previous chapters. For example, if you decide that your boss is a Brainy type, you should slow down and focus on the facts instead of making quick decisions. Try it a few times and consider the reaction. If you get positive responses, you're on the right track. If not, review the information and try again.

UNDERSTANDING OTHERS QUIZ

For each set of questions, circle the two letterss next to the response that most closely describes how the person acts at work.

This person is more likely to:

1) B   C   Discuss feelings

               OR

    A   D   Discuss facts

2) C   D   Talk in a group meeting

               OR

    A   B   Be quiet in a group meeting

3) B C   Smile often and use other facial expressions
             OR
   A D   Use limited facial expressions

4) C D   Often interrupt others when they're speaking
             OR
   A B   Rarely interrupt others when they're speaking

5) B C   Spend time with other people
             OR
   A D   Spend time by herself

6) C D   Make statements
             OR
   A B   Ask questions

7) B C   Share information about her personal life and
             family
             OR
   A D   Not share personal and family information

8) C D   Usually talk quickly with few pauses
             OR
   A B   Usually talk slowly and include pauses

9) A B   Give information in subtle or indirect ways
             OR
   C D   Give information in direct ways

10A D   Rely on logic
             OR
   B C   Rely on intuition or "gut feelings"

Add up all the responses:

A: ☐ Brainy

B: ☐ Buddy

C: ☐ Bubbly

D: ☐ Bossy

Total should = 20. If not, go back and review your answers.

The scores will give you an idea of where the other person is comfortable and where they're not. This information can help you to determine how to best deal with her.

EXAMPLE

If you score your manager:

Bossy — 2

Bubbly — 10

Buddy — 8

Brainy — 0

These scores show that she is most comfortable with Bubbly and Buddy type information. In order to communicate with her better, you would want to deal with her in a friendly way. These scores also show that you wouldn't want to focus on using only logic and facts to persuade her. It would be better to talk about how other people feel. By scoring how you see her communicate, you have a good idea of what you should do and what you should avoid.

For more information on how to deal with each of the communication types, you should review the chapters on your communication type to see tips for dealing with others. It can also be helpful to read the chapters that describe the types you're trying to deal with so you can understand them better.

17   Plan for the Future

The information in this book is part of an ongoing process for you to increase your success at work. You can't just learn how to do it and forget about it. You need to keep practicing. And the more you practice, the more comfortable it will be for you. When you are very comfortable with the information, you will find that you barely need to think about it; communicating differently becomes second nature.

Should you use this information when you communicate with everyone? You might as well ask, if you know four different languages, should you speak to people in their native languages or should you force them to speak in your native language? When you become fluent in a second language, you can easily use it when you need to speak. With practice, you can become fluent in the language of different communication types and use them to communicate better with everyone.

You already take personal preferences into account when you communicate with other people. For example, if you know that your boss is a golf nut, you probably make an effort to talk to her about golf. If you know that your biggest customer loves Italian food, don't you pick Italian restaurants when you go out for business dinners? Using this communication information is just taking it a step further.

When you get new information about someone else, remember to expand the way you think about them. Just as you are a multi-faceted person, so are all the people you come into contact with during your work life. And if you can learn to deal with them in a way that makes them more comfortable and productive, you'll be much more successful.

DEALING WITH CHANGE

Change is a constant part of life and work. One of the best ways to prepare for the future is to increase your flexibility when you deal with others. In today's fast-paced environment, you know change is inevitable: your boss moves to a different department, your co-worker gets fired or your main customer gets replaced by someone else in their company. It's not easy when you need to work with new people; however, practicing your flexibility can help you to be prepared for the future.

For example, if you are a Brainy type and so is your boss, you will be rewarded for attention to details and following procedures. But what happens if your boss leaves and you have to report to a Bubbly type? Suddenly the Bubbly type doesn't like the things about your work that your previous boss liked. She complains that you just aren't friendly enough and you spend too much time focusing on the details. If you find that's happening, then it's time to use the information in this book to see how you can better deal with her.

WHAT IF I FEEL PHONY?

You might be reluctant to use some of this information because it may feel phony to you. Don't use anything that makes you feel uncomfortable or that you don't think is right for you. For example, if you are a Bossy type working with a Bubbly type and you don't genuinely want to be friendlier with her, then don't. You can use some of the other suggestions instead, such as encouraging her creative ideas. This communication information should only be used when you have a genuine desire to get better results with others. If not, other people will see through it and you'll cause problems for yourself.

WHY DOESN'T THE INFORMATION WORK ALL THE TIME?

People are individuals so they don't react in predictable ways. In addition, all of the people whom you work with are combinations of the different types. Even though most people have one way of communicating that is the most natural for them, they may switch to their secondary type occasionally, especially under stress. For example, a Bubbly type that also has characteristics of a Brainy type may tend to get very quiet when she is under a big strain at work.

WHY JUST ME?

You may also be wondering why you have to do all this work. Why can't the other people whom you work with learn this information too? They can. You can share this information with them so they can try to communicate with you in a way you like. Remember though that you can only change your behavior. The other person may not be willing or may not be able to make changes. If you feel it's not fair for you to do all this work, ask yourself, "Do I want communication to be better with this person?" If the answer is "yes" then it's worth it for you to go to the trouble of making some small changes.

DEALING WITH GROUPS

So far, we have talked about how to deal with individuals. When you need to deal with a group of different communication types, you may have a tendency to slip back to the way that feels most natural. If you do, you'll only be communicating well with people that are like you. The best way to communicate clearly with a group of people is to make sure that you include information for each of the communication types. For example if you have to turn in a report to a committee you should include:

For the Bossy type:
✓A one page overview with bullet points (so she doesn't have to spend time reading the entire report).

For the Bubbly type:
✓Motivating information in the report that shows why she should be excited about this or how this creatively solves a problem.

For the Buddy type:
✓Information on how this will affect people. You might also want to include how people feel about it.

For the Brainy type:
✓Step-by-step information on how this will work, as well as procedures. It can also be helpful if you include detailed charts and graphs in an appendix to show how you assembled the information as well as historical data.

If you are making a presentation to a group you should:

For the Bossy type:
✓Include a quick overview and focus on bottom-line results.

For the Bubbly type:
✓Include some humor or make the presentation fun with colorful overheads.

For the Buddy type:
✓Include information on how people feel about the topic.

For the Brainy type:

✓Include process information and explain step-by-step how you came to your conclusions. You may also want to have reference material to hand out that includes details you don't plan to cover in the presentation.

Understanding Bossy types, Bubbly types, Buddy types and Brainy types can help you to understand how people are different from you. You can learn to appreciate others for who they are even when their approaches to communication are strange to you.

This information also helps you recognize how people see you. It lets you determine what changes you would like to make in the ways you deal with others so you can get better results.

If you are only able to communicate in one primary way, you will only be comfortable with people who are like you. That leaves out a large part of the population. In addition, the best way to get new ideas is to work with people that are not the same as you.

When you started reading this book, what were the results that you hoped to get? Did you want to get along better with others, learn a step-by-step process for better communication, get other people to do what you want or have more fun? You can do all of this by making small changes in the way you interact with people. If people see you in just one way it will limit you. When others see you as flexible, you open up many more opportunities to be successful. You can't change other people, but you can change yourself to get better results.

By understanding how you can communicate with different kinds of people, you can be more successful.

FINAL RECOMMENDATIONS:

Bossy type—Do it.

Bubbly type—Have fun and go for it!

Buddy type—Use this information to really get to know other people and to help them to feel more comfortable when working with you.

Brainy type—Take your time and plan how you're going to use this information.

Appendix

Appendix

Appendix - How to Determine Communication Types

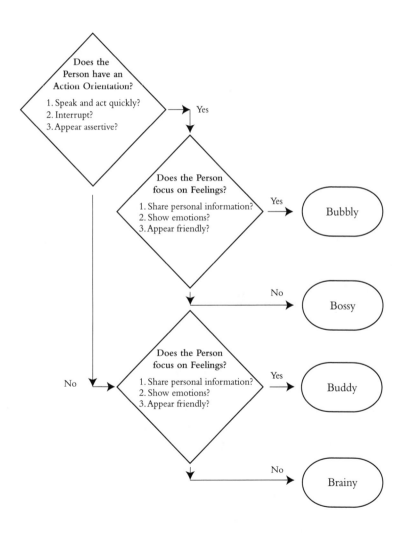

To subscribe to the Bossy, Bubbly, Buddy, Brainy newsletter or for more information go to www.inyourfaceink.com.

Give the Gift of Communication to Your Friends and Colleagues

Check Your Leading Bookstore or Order Here

YES, I want ___copies of Why Can't **You** Communicate Like **Me**? at $15.95 each, plus $4 shipping per book (Arizona residents please add $1.40 sales tax per book). Allow 15 days for delivery For credit card sales or for large order discounts, go to www.inyourfaceink.com.

My check or money order for $_____is enclosed.

Name_____

Company_____

Address_____

City/State/Zip_____

Phone_____

Email_____

Please make your check payable and return to:

In Your Face Ink, LLC
9524 W. Camelback Rd. #130-182
Glendale, AZ 85305
Email: admin@inyourfaceink.com